AUTHOR'S NOTE

The book you are about to read is an unauthorized work of narrative nonfiction. Similar in definition to historical fiction and creative nonfiction, narrative nonfiction is a style of writing that presents factual information shaped and presented to read like fiction. As a dramatization of real events, artistic license is employed at times to combine incidents that occurred on separate occasions into a single cohesive 'scene' for the sake of dramatic brevity and flow. In addition, dramatic license allows for the author to occasionally speculate on dialogue or how particular events are affecting the subject internally. Although much of what the book subject's mother experienced in the concentration camps is known and documented, gaps in her story do exist; in such instances, real stories of other Holocaust survivors have been inserted to flesh out and provide proper historical dimension to the vignette in question. Please see 'Source Notes' to satisfy concerns regarding accuracy of topics covered in these pages as the overwhelming majority are taken straight from the subject's own autobiographies and interviews spanning 38 years.

PRAISE FOR *"GENE SIMMONS: A ROCK N ROLL JOURNEY IN THE SHADOW OF THE HOLOCAUST"*

"Impressive and thorough research make this a most valuable book on a distinctively Jewish American story".

-Rabbi Simcha Weinstein
Author: "Up Up and Oy Vey : How Jewish History, Culture and Values Shaped the Comic Book Superhero"

"I am honored to be included in this inspirational endeavor that celebrates the life of one of the legendary figures of Rock and Roll and American pop culture and his mother, both, as true survivors in the shadows of the Holocaust."

-Bill Starkey
Founder: The KISS Army

"Ross Berg's work is an amazing accomplishment. He has researched and created an in-depth and thorough look into the life and mind of Gene Simmons. Through his amazing insight, Ross gives us a glimpse of what few before have managed: a genuine look behind the mask."

-Ken Mills
Co-Founder: The PodKISSt

"Going back through the life of Gene Simmons, to his humble beginnings, really gives one a new respect for the man."

-Cynthia Nash Sebring
Member: KISS Army Florida

"Ross Berg's amazing book equals standards of scientific research. It is an enormous resource and highly satisfying in the sense that I know I can refer to it any time for unique insights on Gene's life".

-Giedrius Audrius
Founding Member: The KISS Detention Hall

"It's great that someone has dug a little deeper into Gene's past in order to discover what has given him the drive to do what he does for nearly four decades."

-Austin
Vocalist of "The StarChild Songbook:
The Music of Paul Stanley from KISS"

"This book comes at an important time in history when Israel's sovereignty is most threatened."

- Gordon G.G. Gebert
Author: "KISS & Tell"

"In this speculative account, Ross Berg traces the Demon's origins to the darkest chapter in human history and compels us never to forget it."

-Stephen Lord
Founder- Crime Writers of South Australia

"Only through a study of where Gene has come from can we get a glimpse of what made him the man he is today."

-Dale Sherman
Author: "Black Diamond –
The Unofficial Biography of KISS"

"I cannot even begin to imagine the horrors that Flora and so many other victims of Hitler went through; I know it impacted Gene's life a great deal. Flora and Gene deserve not only this book but any and all other tributes that come their way."

-David Campbell
Founder: KISS Army Kansas

"This is a story of how out of the misery and death of the Holocaust, life sprang forth. Loud, spitting, fire-breathing life."

-Jim Hagerman, Graphic Artist

"The term "Real KISS fan" is often thrown around amongst the KISS Army. Without a doubt, Ross Berg is one of those fans. I've known Ross for a number of years now and it has been a pleasure. During this time we have developed quite the friendship and his support of PodKISSt has meant the world to us over the past 4 years. For that, I am forever grateful and extremely proud of what Ross has done with this book. Ross' road to writing this book has not always been easy. Some KISS fans have criticized Ross for digging deeper into Flora's experiences in the Holocaust and in raising the young Chaim, but he persevered. His persistence has paid off. Gene took notice and featured the "Flora Army" on his television show and interest has surged. Finally, Ross is getting to share a part of the KISS legacy that, for so long, has been shrouded in mystery. We hear a lot about the formation of the band, the various albums, and the backstage politics; but no one has ever really delved into the tragedies that affected the formation of KISS until now. Ross has done that here. This book is a riveting look at how Gene's and Flora's experiences earlier in their lives shaped the image and music of Gene Simmons and KISS as a whole. A connection that most would have never thought to uncover. A story that shapes the art that KISS fans around the world have enjoyed for nearly 40 years. A story for "Real KISS fans" written by the ultimate KISS fan."

-James Hager
Co-Founder: The PodKISSt

"Ross Berg's work is a true labor of love. His determination and commitment has led to a heartfelt and inspirational work that conveys a wealth of emotions that will tug at your heartstrings."

-Lisa Jackson
Freelance Writer/Former Television Writer/
Newspaper Reporter

"Ross Berg has written a thoughtful book about Gene Simmons that includes a memorable account of how his mother's experiences in the Holocaust helped shape his sensibility. It's important that we never forget those experiences and ensure against such horrors ever being repeated."

-John Swenson
Author: 'KISS – Headliners'

an unauthorized work of narrative nonfiction

GENE SIMMONS: A ROCK 'N' ROLL JOURNEY IN THE SHADOW OF THE HOLOCAUST

ROSS BERG
FOUNDER OF "THE FLORA ARMY"
AS SEEN ON THE A&E NETWORK SERIES
GENE SIMMONS FAMILY JEWELS

Mill City Press

Copyright © 2012 by Ross Berg.

Mill City Press, Inc.
212 3rd Avenue North, Suite 290
Minneapolis, MN 55401
612.455.2294
www.millcitypublishing.com

This book or any portion thereof may not be reproduced or used in any manner whatsoever without the express written permission of the publisher except for the use of brief quotations in a book review.

All rights reserved. No part of this publication may be reproduced, stored in a retrieval system, or transmitted, in any form or by any means, electronic, mechanical, photocopying, recording, or otherwise, without the prior written permission of the author.

ISBN-13: 978-1-937600-58-7
LCCN: 2011943973

Cover Design and Typeset by Nate Meyers

Printed in the United States of America

FOR MARCELA
~ The Love Of My Life ~

"Although the Jews were the main target of the Holocaust, every human being is a victim, because those Jews who were murdered, and their never-to-be-born progeny, might have done so much for humankind. The realization that the victimization will never end is the best reason we must never forget."

-Alan Dershowitz
Author: "In Defense of Israel"
American Lawyer, Jurist, and Political Commentator

"Often, during my speaking engagements, I mention that one of my core activities in life is to keep alive the memory of the innocent victims of the Holocaust, which I do through my writings and lectures. They should never be forgotten."

– Magda Herzberger
Writer/Holocaust Survivor

"Gene Simmons is living proof that the tragedy of the Holocaust only made people of the Jewish faith stronger."

-Peppy Castro
KISS Songwriting Collaborator

"I wish there were no cultural barriers in this world but since there are, let Rock and Roll bring us all together - especially for those who are incapable of letting go of their judgments. Through music we can love the world together."

-Wendy Moore
Author: "Into The Void With Ace Frehley"

PREFACE

In 1977, I was eight years old. One day at temple they brought all of us kids into a large auditorium and dimmed the lights. My brother, aged 10, was sitting next to me as a film rolled. The movie began with pictures of Israel and Rabbis and Purim carnivals and such. Suddenly, there was this bizarre footage of these incredibly skinny and dirty people all huddled together in what looked like a barn full of bunk beds. Up to that point in my life, at the age of 8, I really wasn't aware of any genuine tragedies in the world - I just knew that these weird, boney people they were showing looked funny to me. And I started laughing. Loudly. Suddenly, the lights went on and the film was stopped. A woman who worked at the temple and looked to be about 100 years old to me when I was a child, came marching angrily down the auditorium aisle and demanded to know who was laughing. I could feel myself shaking with fear as she came closer to where I was sitting. "Who was laughing!" she yelled. I was scared to death and remained silent -- too frightened to admit that it was I who had laughed at the alien-looking people in the movie. After a few more minutes, she marched back up the aisle - fuming with anger - and the film resumed. My brother looked over to me with a disappointed expression. 'What had I done wrong', I wondered to myself. When the film was over and all of us children were leaving the auditorium, my brother said he needed to talk to me about something. He revealed to me that there were certain people in the world who hated us because we were Jews. My eyes widened. I couldn't believe what he was telling me. People hate us? Why? My brother said that those people in the movie were Jews that were enslaved and killed simply because they were Jewish. I'll never forget that day, for many reasons. But mostly because from that day until the present moment - my life as a Jew has essentially been defined by the Holocaust. Strange, certainly, as Judaism existed long before Adolph Hitler was ever born; but I can't seem to get around it. To me, being Jewish has meant that I belong to a group of people who survived - and didn't survive - the Nazi death camps. My mother's parents fled Germany just in time. Though they were lucky not to have ended up in the Camps, the rest of my mother's family on her father's side did, and all but one perished. The sole surviving uncle came to live in my mother's house when she was a child. She ran her fingers along the numbers on his arm, and felt the loss of his presence when he often withdrew in silence at the dinner table. He had once had a wife and children at his own dinner table. While my maternal father's side of the family was being annihilated, my maternal mother's side endured completely different experiences. Though my mother's mother had converted to Judaism, her family was not Jewish. One of my mother's uncles served in the Hitler Youth, and two of her cousins fought for Germany against the Allied Forces. The remainder of the relatives were often starving and endured the bombings on Berlin.

The complexity of my family living on two sides of the Holocaust has contributed to my struggle with this dark chapter of history. The impact of the Holocaust on individuals at that time continues down through the next generations. Growing up, my mother never discussed the Holocaust with her parents. It was an unwritten rule, as is common. Only one personal incident was ever related by my mom's mother; it involved a time just before leaving Germany. My grandparents hung on to each other and shook in their bed as the Gestapo dragged off a man from the next apartment in the middle of the night. Knowing of the fear, suffering and loss they had endured, created tremendous anxiety in my mother who wished to always protect them and make them happy. She consequently grew up with a fair amount of her own fears, and the fact that her mother was overprotective. My mom wasn't allowed to learn to ride a bike or babysit because: "Something might happen!". My grandmother's explanation was that she wanted to keep my mother safe at all costs. At the end of his life, my grandfather became bedridden and delusional. My mother calls this "The Hitler Period". He would scream in his bed in German: "They're coming. They're going to kill us!" This from a man who never once spoke of the Holocaust in my mother's presence.....perhaps in no one's presence. All that terror which had been squashed down was unleashed again and again during that time. My mother, like many children of survivors, felt the need to make up for what happened. She dated Jewish boys and married my father, a Jew. She made sure her parents had grandchildren...physical evidence that Hitler didn't accomplish what he had set out to do. She taught Religious School for years, and faithfully studies the Torah, often thinking of those who were never given that opportunity. She gathers us all up to celebrate the holidays, to both create memories that bind us together and traditions she hopes will outlive her. And she has spent most of her adult life in the service of others as a psychotherapist with a PhD, specializing in Loss and Grief. She taught a college course for years on "Dying and Death". My mother, like Gene Simmons, is a 'Child of the Holocaust'. The offspring of a Holocaust victim. A survivor of a survivor. There are many shared traits amongst Children of the Holocaust. A good number of these characteristics drive and guide the content of this book. An example is Gene's intense motivation to succeed and survive in the face of any obstacle -- feeling that his accomplishments must be huge and his life lived to the fullest in order to make up for those whose lives and accomplishments were cut so tragically short.

Gene's mother survived the Holocaust but the rest of her family perished in the camps. As the Child of a Holocaust survivor, Gene was anxious to understand what his mother had experienced in the Concentration Camps; but those events were too painful for her to talk about. As such, a young Gene was forced to collect bits and pieces and fragments of information on his own about the Holocaust and the Nazis that killed his mother's entire family. But the events still remained cloaked in mystery as nothing was ever directly discussed with the young boy. Due to the mysteriousness of the atrocious events, it is perhaps only natural that Gene would 'play' at being evil in an attempt to understand and even control his curiosities about the dark side. Repressed thoughts, fears, and personal demons have a way of eventually bubbling to the surface and, for Gene, those thoughts, fears, and personal demons gushed to the forefront of his being in the form of a hideous, fire-breathing, blood-spewing, death-mask creation that he began building as a young child in Haifa, Israel.

Gene came to America from Israel as a young boy unable to speak English. He was taunted by the other children for his language difficulties and for wearing his yarmulke to school. He was an outcast based on how different he was from the other children and soon became a loner consumed with escaping his unhappiness through his own imagination. Gene withdrew into his mind – into a world of fantasy where he could transform himself from an unpopular boy from Israel to an exciting comic book hero or menacing horror movie monster.

Years later, Gene would infuse this childhood pain into songs like "Mr. Make Believe (Let Me Live Inside You)", "A World Without Heroes", "In My Head (Look Behind The Mask)", "Only You", "Childhood's End" and "Within"; songs that emphasized the importance of heroes and examined the universal need to hide behind 'masks' and alter-egos when the pain of the real world becomes too much to bear.

It was a sad and lonely childhood; and yet it was this very pain and the coping strategies employed to combat the hurt that led a young child from Israel born to a survivor of the Nazi Holocaust to emerge as one of the most compelling and complex entertainers of our time.

Gene Simmons is a very important person to me. As a child, I witnessed a black and white photo of Gene in a magazine and my world turned to color.

Gene inspired me to begin writing songs.

To learn the bass guitar.

To sing and play in bands.

To study art, comic books, and film noir.

To believe in myself.
To further my knowledge of the Holocaust.
To be proud to be a Jew.

People look at me strange when they find out how much my life has been affected by Gene Simmons. They can't believe the 'museum' of band merchandise I've collected since the 1970's. They are amazed at the vast number of rare Fanzines I have amassed -- all created by Gene in his mother's home as a teenager. I have often been told that I don't 'look' like a KISS fan -- and yet that is really the point….and Gene taught us the lesson well: it's not about the outer mask, it's about what's going on in your mind -- an inner world of make-believe, fantasy, and dreams…..

As a child, I had KISS sleepover parties with friends and plastered the walls of my bedroom with photos of the band.

As a teenager, I purchased a black bass guitar and set about teaching myself to play like Gene.

As a college student, I played in bands and performed KISS tunes.

As an adult, husband, and father -- I worked as a Moderator for KISSOnline, started several Gene Simmons websites, self-published a book about KISS' "Elder" album, and celebrated my 40th birthday with a 'Gene Simmons Party' – proof that the more things change the more they stay the same.

The genesis and odyssey of "The Flora Army" goes back to Gene's first book; an autobiography called 'KISS And Make-Up'. I had read things about

Gene's mother here and there in interviews over the years -- but this was the first time I had an opportunity to fully digest her harrowing and courageous story as a Holocaust survivor. The pictures contained in the book revealed Gene's mother Flora to be an extremely beautiful woman. I wanted to know more. I was inspired. Perhaps Flora's story of survival could educate a whole segment of the population who had never known or cared about the Holocaust before. Six million is a hard number to comprehend. Putting a face to the Shoah – an Anne Frank or a Flora Klein – can often better convey the realness of the tragedy to the next generation.

I felt I had stumbled upon a unique thesis of sorts: in what ways had the Holocaust affected the life and art of Gene Simmons?

Flora, of course, would be a prominent figure within such a study.

In certain ways, Flora's strength and fortitude reminded me of my German Grandmother. My Grandmother who had gotten us out of Germany just before Hitler put his deadly plans into action. The Grandmother I loved and missed so dearly since her death in the 1990's. I wanted to tell this story for her as well.

After working as a Moderator under the wise leadership of Michael Brandvold for KISS' official website "KISSOnline", I spent some time helping the amazingly knowledgable Julian Gill moderate his site – "The KISS Faq".

Julian's computer smarts and essential 'KISS Album Focus' book series inspired me to strike out on my own as both a Webmaster and an author.

With the help of my dear friend Leanne St. Germaine – creator of the much respected "Paul Stanley's Paradise" webpage -- I was soon running my own website devoted to Gene, his childhood, his mother, his Fanzine creations from the 60's, the Holocaust, the history of Jews and the comic book industry, personality traits in Children of the Holocaust, and more. That webpage, called 'Almost Human', came to serve as the basic outline for this book.

As my research into Gene's childhood and Flora's life intensified, I decided to create "The Flora Army"; a fond tip of the hat to "The KISS Army" Fan Club founded by a trailblazing young man named Bill Starkey in the 70's. Initially little more than a logo, "The Flora Army" was something I began to take public on several KISS-related Discussion Forums. I would start topics concerning the teenage life of Gene Simmons and post rare photos of Flora in Israel from the 1940's.

The response I got to the majority of these topics was anemic and I soon added the catch-phrase "An Army of One" to the logo as a good-natured, self-deprecating poke at myself. But I refused to give up. I believed in the power and the importance of what I was doing.

Around this time, I had the incredible opportunity to meet Mr. Simmons at a book signing. As I was trying to explain to him all that he had meant to me in my life, and that my mother had also been a child of survivors, my two month old daughter began to cry. Gene immediately and lovingly turned his attentions to my daughter and entwined his pinky finger with hers. As my daughter stopped crying, Gene took me aside and gently explained to me that his mother Flora often used this same trick to get him to stop crying when he was a baby. This was obviously just one of the many special coping methods and survival techniques that Flora had passed on to Gene and his eyes lit up as he spoke of her. I felt so privileged to have Gene reveal to me one of Flora's parenting secrets. I took it as a bit of a sign. I had to keep moving forward. I had to write this book.

One morning, it came to my attention that Nick Simmons was going to be signing his new comic book at 'Meltdown Comics' on Sunset Boulevard in Los Angeles. I printed out a working copy of my book cover - listed my contact information on the reverse side, grabbed my camera, and headed out. Nick was shy but friendly and graciously signed his comic book with a shiny silver pen and posed for a picture with me and my two young children. 'Well, thank you for coming out', his manager said. I mustered up my courage and clutched the print-out I had brought with me. I leaned in to speak a little more personally with Nick. The 'Gene Simmons Family Jewels' film crew had a camera pointed directly in our faces. "Nick, I am writing a book about your father's childhood, and........" Before I could get the rest of my sentence out, Nick excitedly took the copy of the book cover from me and examined it with great interest. I finally broke in: "Well, because the book deals with your father's childhood – I was hoping that I could interview Florence for the book. Is there anything you could do to help me to make that interview happen? All of my contact information is on the reverse side." Nick pondered my request for a moment and then said, smiling" Wait.....you wanna talk to my Grandmother? Gosh, I don't know if I can help you with *that* one". Nick again studied the paper I had given him. "I'll tell you what. Can I take this home with me?", he asked. 'Absolutely', I answered. "I'll take this home with me. But I'm not promising anything....." "All my information is on the back", I reminded him. We shook hands and I went on my way.

Months passed and I heard nothing from Gene's camp about the book. I was disappointed but continued to work on my project day and night.

During this period, I discovered "Facebook" and decided to bring 'The Flora Army' to this new social networking juggernaut. Once again, I filled my page with information about Gene, his childhood, his mother, his Fanzine creations from the 60's, the Holocaust, the history of Jews and the comic book industry, and personality traits in Children of the Holocaust. I posted sample chapter 'vignettes' from my book-in-progress and continued to try to educate others about the Holocaust and the heroic life of Flora Klein. Slowly, people began to take interest and I amassed a following of about 100 followers. One day, out of the blue, a cheerful woman named Valerie Young contacted me. She is the Webmistress of the official "Fans of Shannon Tweed" group page on Facebook; Shannon being Gene's girlfriend of nearly 30 years and the mother of his two children. Shannon asked Valerie to link my "Flora Army" page to the "Fans of Shannon Tweed" Facebook group – essentially giving it her blessing. I could not believe it. My mind wandered back to Nick Simmons bringing my book proposal home to his parents – Gene and Shannon – and selling them on its merits. This was just the beginning of a multitude of dreams to come true.

Later that month on genesimmons.com, Gene's official website, news began to spread that Gene was to visit Anne Frank's home in Amsterdam for the Season Six Premiere of his popular 'Gene Simmons Family Jewels' television show on the A&E Network. Busy planning my 4 year old son's birthday party – I hadn't paid much attention to Facebook in a couple of weeks. When I finally did log on, there was a mysterious message from a user named Adam Freeman announcing the following on my page: "The 'Flora Army' is going to be featured on Gene's tv show next Sunday night." I thought for sure this individual was pulling my leg and I didn't even respond to the post. A week went by and I kept seeing Adam Freeman's message on my page. Highly skeptical, I finally responded with: "Do you mean Flora herself is going to appear on Gene's tv show or the program is literally going to spotlight my 'Flora Army' Facebook page?"

"Yes", wrote Adam, "Gene's tv show is going to showcase your 'Flora Army' site exclusively". "How do you know this?" I inquired. "Because I am the Executive Producer of Gene's television show", Adam replied. "Trust me. 'The Flora Army' is going to be on Gene's tv show this Sunday." Now I was shaking in my boots. I know how rabidly protective Gene is of his mother and I started to fear the worst: what if Gene was going to feature my Facebook page on his show in order to mock my site and blast me as an example of an 'unstable fan'? I voiced these concerns to Adam – but he assured me that Gene was 'very honored' by what I had done and wanted to display my good works for the world to see. Adam Freeman was as nice, professional, and caring as could be and – while I believed him and his reassurances – I was a nervous wreck while watching Gene's television program that night.

At the conclusion of an extremely touching episode where Gene visited the Anne Frank home and spoke with a local family who had been touched by the Holocaust – photos and content from my 'Flora Army' site began to fill the screen as Gene's family spoke the following words…..

Nick: "Apparently there's a Facebook fan page for Grandma called THE FLORA ARMY."

Sophie: "It's a group of dad's fans who are now Grandma's fans who have a Facebook page just for Grandma and everything Grandma does."

Shannon: "I love the pictures."

Nick: "And I guess they read dad's book, it tells about her and they say it's honoring this courageous woman - and I was like.....*really*....I didn't expect that, but ummm........it's cool!"

I cannot begin to explain the complete feeling of shock and warmth I felt throughout my entire body at that moment. This was a man who had affected every aspect of my life in such a profound manner since I was a small child – and now I was affecting his, in some small way, nearly 40 years later.

Within hours, membership on 'The Flora Army' Facebook page shot up to 25,000 members.

The following week, Gene's Webmistress Kristy Fuchs was kind enough to forward my thank you letter to Gene and he promptly posted it on his site for all to see:

"Dear Gene – my name is Ross Berg and I started THE FLORA ARMY on Facebook. I want to thank you and your family *so much* for acknowledging my site on your show last night. I hope you will check in on the page once in a while because people are saying the most wonderful things about you and your beautiful mother Flora. God bless you and your entire family. You made my wish come true by helping to spread the word about the Holocaust and how each new generation *must* be informed so that nothing like this ever happens again. Ross"

The next day Gene posted on his 'Twitter' account: "A kind thank you to all of you who are saying nice things about my Mother on "The Flora Army".

As of this writing, Gene Simmons is in the midst of visiting Israel; to the hospital where he was born, the Café where Flora once worked, to the Yad Vashem Holocaust Museum. In recent press conferences - Gene has declared Israel, definitively, as his true home. After 61 years, it appears the little boy from Haifa has come full circle in his return to the Holy Land.

Events have come full circle in my life as well. The little eight year old boy who learned of the Holocaust that day in Temple is now the father of an eight year old child.

It is my wish for that child to learn of her Jewish heritage and the facts of the Holocaust in a manner quite different from what I experienced in that darkened auditorium so many years ago. It is my hope that both of my children grow to see their religion as something glorious and beautiful; to learn of the Holocaust without allowing it to define their entire notion of Judaism. It is my dream to educate and alert the next generation to the horrors of the Shoah so that such an atrocity is never permitted to occur again.

To educate the next generation.

The responsibility is in our hands.

I present to you this book about a mother and a son. Let their story of strength and survival inspire and their darkest tragedies move you to educate your children.

> Ross Berg
> Northridge, California
> November 2011

The author's German Grandmother who
saved the family from Hitler and the Nazis
(photo courtesy of the Berg Family)

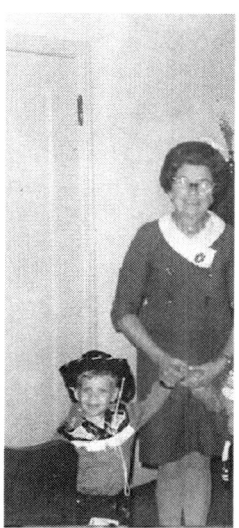

The author as a boy with his
German Grandmother
(photo courtesy of the author)

The author meeting his hero, Gene Simmons, at various signings throughout the years
(photos courtesy of the author)

Gene Simmons

Gene Simmons using his mother Florence's "Pinky Technique" to get the author's daughter to stop crying - - - it worked!
(photos courtesy of the author)

Meeting with Nick Simmons to discuss the possibility of an interview with his Grandmother Florence for this book

(photo courtesy of the author)

"Florence's gripping story, enduring the death camps of Nazi Germany, chronicles her personal fortitude and indomitable will to survive. She began life a second time in Israel after the camps were liberated, and then again when she came to America with her young son. Florence's sacrifice and struggle embody what it means to be a survivor and ultimately triumph."

-Christopher Lendt
Author: "KISS And Sell: The Making Of A Supergroup"
Former KISS Business Manager

"I worked with Kiss as a PR person in 1976-77, as a Manager in the nineteen-eighties, and as the President of Mercury Records in the early nineties. Gene's mother Florence was always a fixture in his life. She was the ultimate Gene Simmons fan and for years kept scrapbooks about all of his achievements. Gene adored her. Her vibrance and passion for life and pride in Gene was and is one of the great life-affirming relationships I have ever seen in light of the brutality and evil she had to confront earlier in her life as a victim of the Holocaust."

-Danny Goldberg
Author: "Bumping Into Geniuses - My Life Inside The Rock and Roll Business"

"When I think about the Jewish experience, one word that comes to mind is perseverance. Perseverance is demonstrated by Moses standing up to Pharaoh pleading for the freedom of the Hebrews from Goshen. Perseverance is demonstrated by Flora Klein daily surviving in the Concentration Camp during the Nazi Regime. Perseverance is demonstrated by Gene Simmons who has taken the life lessons taught to him by his mother and made it a way of life."

-Adam Nierenberg
Co-Administrator: The Flora Army Facebook Site

timeline and points of interest

- In 1904, Theodore Herzl - Leader of the Zionist Political Movement - seeks Rome's blessing on Jewish aspirations to reclaim their ancient land; Pope Pius X refuses, stating: "The Jews have not recognised our Lord, therefore we cannot recognise the Jewish people."

- In 1927, Florence (Flora) Klein is born in Jund, Hungary

- In 1937, Israel accepts a proposal for a two-state system in order to achieve peace in the Middle East; the Arab government refuses the offer

- In 1939, German Dictator Adolph Hitler orders his troops to invade Poland; World War II begins

- In 1939, United States President Franklin D. Roosevelt refuses to allow 20,000 Jewish children to enter America as they seek to flee Nazi persecution

- In 1939, Nazi Leader Heinrich Himmler works with Palestine to lay the groundwork for genocidal death camps in the Middle East to further solve 'The Jewish Problem'

- In 1941, Flora Klein is sent to a Nazi Concentration Camp

- In 1944, Pope Pius XII agrees to save thousands of Jews during the Holocaust; on the condition that they have already converted to Catholicism or are Jewish children actively being groomed for conversion by Catholic families

- In 1945, Germany surrenders to the Russians and World War II concludes; Adolph Hitler commits suicide in his underground bunker

- In 1946, Flora Klein meets Yechiel Witz at a Zionist Youth Group event

- In 1947, Flora Klein and Yechiel Witz are married

- In 1948, Israel is recognized as a Jewish State by the United Nations; the next day it is attacked by Arab armies for Egypt, Syria, and Jordan

- In 1949, Flora Klein gives birth to a son named Chaim Witz in Haifa, Israel

- In 1955, Flora Klein and Yechiel Witz are divorced

- In 1957, Flora Klein and Chaim Witz come to America and settle in Queens, New York; Chaim Witz changes his name to Gene Klein

- In 1959, Gene Klein studies at a Jewish Yeshiva and dreams of becoming a Rabbi

- In 1960, Gene Klein purchases his first copy of "Famous Monsters of Filmland"; issue #6 featuring King Kong cover art

- In 1962, Gene Klein becomes a Bar Mitzvah

- In 1963, Gene Klein begins to write and publish his own Sci Fi/Monster/Fantasy Fanzines with the mimeograph machine purchased for him by his mother Flora Klein

- In 1964, Flora Klein buys her son Gene Klein his first guitar

- In 1967, the "Six-Day War" begins when Egypt closes the Gulf of Aqaba in order to halt Israeli shipping

- In 1969, Gene Klein writes "I Am A New Man"; a song acknowledging that the composer began his life during a time of ruin in history

- In 1969, Gene Klein writes "Amen Corner"; a song owing its title to a prayer ritual

- In 1969, Gene Klein writes "My Uncle Is A Raft"; a song of appreciation for the composer's Uncle Larry who welcomed he and his mother Flora Klein into his home when they first arrived to America from Israel. Uncle Larry seemed to fill a much needed father-role for Gene at the time

- In 1969, Gene Klein writes "My Mother Is The Most Beautiful Woman In The World"; a song devoted to the woman who gave the composer life and was his greatest protector, Flora Klein

- In 1970, Gene Klein graduates from Richmond College and becomes an Elementary School Teacher

- In 1970, Gene Klein writes "Goin' Blind"; a song examining the pain of being different

- In 1973, Gene Klein changes his name to Gene Simmons and forms the rock band KISS with Rhythm Guitarist Paul Stanley, Lead Guitarist Ace Frehley, and Drummer Peter Criss

- In 1973, Egypt and Syria launch a surprise attack on Israel on Yom Kippur

- In 1975, Flora Klein is featured in "People" Magazine

- In 1976, Flora Klein marries Holocaust Survivor Eli Lubowski

- In 1976, Gene Simmons writes "Great Expectations"; a song examining the human desire to see beyond masked identities

- In 1976, London music critics accuse KISS of being Nazis due to their use of the SS lightning bolts in their logo; Gene Simmons defends the band, pointing out that half the group is Jewish

- In 1977, Flora Klein is featured in "People" Magazine

- In 1977, Gene Simmons writes "Almost Human", a song allowing the composer to further explore his monstrous dual identity and alter ego

- In 1978, Gene Simmons begins dating Singer/Actress Cher Bono Allman and declares her his first love

- In 1978, Marvel Comics releases the first KISS Comic Book

- In 1978, Gene Simmons writes "Mr. Make Believe"; a song expressing the composer's desire to hide within a world of fantasy and make believe

- In 1978, Gene Simmons writes "Man of 1,000 Faces"; a song examining the composer's desire to disappear inside a world of make believe and alter egos

- In 1978, Gene Simmons makes his acting debut as his Bat Lizard alter-ego in "KISS Meets The Phantom of the Park"; a made-for-television movie based on the Marvel KISS Comic Book

- In 1979, Flora Klein is featured in "Us" Magazine

- In 1979, Flora Klein is featured in "15 Fever" Magazine

- In 1979, KISS alters their SS lightning bolt logo for German television appearances, concerts and album cover art out of respect for the history of its people

- In 1980, Flora Klein is featured in "People" Magazine

- In 1981, Gene Simmons writes "A World Without Heroes"; a song expressing the composer's love of, and need for, heroes

- In 1981, Gene Simmons writes "Only You"; a song expressing the composer's love of, and need for, heroes

- In 1981, Gene Simmons writes "I"; a song expressing the composer's disdain for drugs and alcohol

- In 1981, KISS releases the concept album "(Music From) The Elder". Based on a short story by Gene Simmons, the action takes place after the Earth has recently recovered from an evil that has nearly destroyed it; a holocaust of sorts

- In 1982, Gene Simmons' Bat Lizard make-up design is trademarked through the United States Patent Office

- In 1983, Gene Simmons appears on the 'Nightwatch' television program to publicly denounce anti-semitic comments made by two Southern Ministers

- In 1984, Gene Simmons begins dating Playboy Model Shannon Tweed; they later have two children together

- In 1986, Flora Klein is featured in "Kerrang!" Magazine

- In 1986, Fred A. Bernstein devotes a chapter to Flora Klein in his book "The Jewish Mother's Hall of Fame"

- In 1986, Gene Simmons plays an Arab Terrorist posing as an Orthodox Rabbi in the feature film "Wanted Dead Or Alive"

- In 1987, Gene Simmons appears in Public Service Announcements denouncing drugs and alcohol

- In 1987, Gene Simmons appears on the David Brenner "Night Life" television program and discusses the interest he had in becoming a Rabbi as a youth

- In 1995, Gene Simmons writes "In My Head"; a song examining the human desire to see beyond masked identities

- In 1995, Gene Simmons writes "Seduction of the Innocent"; a song examining the hypocrisies of the Catholic Church

- In 1995, Gene Simmons writes "I Confess"; a song examining the hypocrisies of the Catholic Church

- In 1995, KISS releases the "Carnival Of Souls" album featuring songs by Gene Simmons questioning the ethics and hypocrisy of the Catholic Church

- In 1996, a study by the 'American Psychiatric Association' reveals that Children of the Holocaust show an increased risk of developing Post-Traumatic Stress Disorder

- In 1997, Image Comics begins a new series of KISS Comic Books

- In 1999, Gene Simmons is featured on the cover of "Famous Monsters of Filmland", Issue #226

- In 2000, Guy Oseary's book "Jews Who Rock" is published and spotlights Gene Simmons as an important Jewish musician alongside the likes of Bob Dylan, Carole King, and Simon & Garfunkel

- In 2001, Flora Klein is featured in the documentary "KISS: Beyond The Make-Up"

- In 2001, Gene Simmons discusses his mother Flora Klein's experiences in the Holocaust in his book "KISS And Make-Up"

- In 2001, Israel offers Palestine a state with its capital in Jerusalem, control over the Temple Mount, a return of roughly 95 percent of the West Bank and the entirety of the Gaza Strip, and a $30 billion dollar compensation package in order to create peace in the Middle East; Palestine refuses the offer

- In 2001, Gene Simmons' father Yechiel Witz passes away in Israel

- In 2002, Dark Horse begins a new series of KISS Comic Books

- In 2003, Scott R. Bernarde's book "Stars Of David" is published and spotlights Gene Simmons as an important Jewish musician alongside the likes of Bob Dylan, Carole King, and Simon & Garfunkel

- In 2003, Gene Simmons discusses his mother Flora Klein's experiences in the Holocaust in his book "Sex, Money, KISS"

- In 2005, Gene Simmons and Flora Klein appear together on the television program "Extra"

- In 2006, Gene Simmons publicly condemns Actor Mel Gibson's anti-semitic tirade in Malibu, CA

- In 2006, the Carnegie Corporation's list of the most prominent foreign-born Americans – "Immigrants: The Pride of America" – includes Gene Simmons as one of the Top 100 Immigrants in America, alongside the likes of Albert Einstein and Henry Kissinger

- In 2006, Gene Simmons appears in the documentary "Look, Up In The Sky! – The Amazing Story of Superman" to discuss Superman's specific links to the Jewish People

- In 2007, KISS Comics Group and Platinum Studios partner to begin a new series of KISS Comic Books

- In 2007, Gene Simmons creates and produces his own comic book series entitled "Gene Simmons House of Horrors"

- In 2008, Gene Simmons discusses his mother Flora Klein's Holocaust experiences on the television program "Shrink Rap"

- In 2010, Gene Simmons visits his childhood home on the television program "Family Jewels" and reminisces about life with his mother Flora Klein

- In 2010, Gene Simmons visits the home of Holocaust victim Anne Frank in Amsterdam; he publicly describes the experience as 'life changing'

- In 2010, Gene Simmons features "The Flora Army" website honoring his mother on his television show 'Gene Simmons Family Jewels'

- In 2010, Gene Simmons features "The Flora Army" website honoring his mother on his official web page GeneSimmons.com

- In 2010, Gene Simmons thanks "The Flora Army" website honoring his mother on his official Twitter page

- In 2010, Gene Simmons is featured on the cover of the monster magazine "Fangoria"

- In 2011, Gene Simmons visits Israel; to the hospital where he was born, the Café where Flora once worked, the Dead Sea, and to the Yad Vashem Holocaust Museum

- In 2011, 'The Flora Army' is the subject of a review in popmatters.com

- In 2011, Gene Simmons declares those who boycott Israel as "fools"

- In 2011, Gene Simmons' visit to Israel is documented in the 'Jewish Journal'

- In 2011, Gene Simmons declares that Israel is, definitively, his true home

- At the time of this writing in November 2011...... KISS have sold over 100 million albums and continue to tour the world. The band is recognized by the RIAA as America's Number One Gold Record Award Winning Group of All Time. In October, Gene married his longtime girlfriend Shannon Tweed. Gene Simmons stars in a reality television show featuring his mother Flora Klein. Flora lives in New York. She is 84 years old.

FOREWORD

'Seth, I Hear You Calling…..'

Gene Klein was an outcast. He was a stranger to America; unfamiliar with the new language and cultural norms of the U.S. His childhood was a solitary one and it was only through art that he eventually connected with a handful of others who shared his passion for comic books and, later on, music. While Gene was creating his sci-fi/horror Fanzine "Cosmos", his new friend Seth Dogramajian was right there with him creating his own Fanzine entitled "Exile". Stephen Coronel, a mutual friend of both young men, often illustrated the covers of these Fanzines and the three formed a strong connection based on their mutual love of fantasy. After The Beatles arrived in America and changed rock and roll forever, Gene and Seth Dogramajian formed bands together with names such as "Lynx", "Rising Sun", and "The Long Island Sounds". When KISS debuted in 1973 and took the world by storm, Gene slowly lost contact with Seth and Stephen. By his own admission, to this day, Gene Simmons is essentially 'friendless'. He has a 40 year working relationship with bandmate Paul Stanley based on mutual respect and admiration – although the two admit they rarely socialize with one another outside of the scope of KISS. Gene has a loving relationship with his partner of close to 30 years, Shannon Tweed – and their two children, Sophie and Nick. He is extremely close to his mother, Florence. He has business partners and acquaintances in the entertainment business but, in the end, remains a loner. That Gene Simmons became a legendary rock icon is a fact, but how he got there – like the stories of all highly successful people in our society – is the result of a multitude of countless serendipitous twists and turns; it *is* fortunate that the young Gene found a way to break out of his shell with the help of two or three peers who related to his love of comic books, monster movies, and rock music - - emboldening him with the confidence and acceptance to forge on and flirt with a career in the entertainment field. One such peer, Seth Dogramajian, has been somewhat of a footnote in the story of Gene's childhood; at least - my hope is - until now. Seth became a friend to Gene at a pivotal time in his life when he was seeking validation and acceptance – and the strength to experiment with the talents he hoped he possessed in the areas of creating comic books and music. Gene needed a sounding board – a friend to stand up on that stage with him and provide the comfort and camaraderie required to perform before an audience of strangers. Seth Dogramajian was that person. He was that friend. Seth's sister Pearl Dogramajian and niece Raina Marie have generously offered to shed some additional light on what made Seth Dogramajian such a special individual for the readers of this book. We thank them for their time and for their memories. Sadly, Seth passed away in 1998 - but he will live on in our hearts and forever be remembered for, amongst many other wonderful things, coaxing a lonely kid named Gene Klein out to play. Seth helped a loner see the possibilities the world had to offer and aided him in finding the courage to take a stab at making his creative dreams a reality. We celebrate Seth Dogramajian for the impact he had on the world. He is anything but a mere footnote.

What follows are Pearl's and Raina's memories of the late great Seth Dogramajian, written exclusively for this book……..

"When Ross asked us to contribute to this project, we were honored to participate. Ross' book reminds us that we grow in the context of multiple environments. In Gene's case, relevant life experiences such as migrating to a foreign country, growing up in the United States during a turbulent period of change, and being the child of a Holocaust survivor all contributed to the development of a rock legend. Ross explores the connection between the Holocaust and Gene's development as an artist and entrepreneur. Gene's music transformed the rock-n-roll industry and mass consciousness, as Gene and KISS have reached iconic status. Gene and KISS went where "no one has gone before" and in doing so created an army of fans."

-Raina Marie
-Pearl Dogramajian

Pearl: "Amidst the backdrop of a diverse Queens community, during the tumultuous 1960's, a group of friends in Joseph Pulitzer junior high school with a shared interest in music, science fiction and art formed a rock band. Practices were often held at my parent's home in Jackson Heights. The main culprits, Gene Klein, Danny Haber, and my brother Seth Dogramajian would take over the living room and create a ruckus - followed by Steve Coronel who would later join the group. They started playing at school functions and then later played at local clubs. As teenagers with an interest in music, they would attend concerts. On one occasion, Seth was responsible for "babysitting" me - his younger sister - and I accompanied Seth, Gene, and Steve to my first concert featuring Janis Joplin, Jimi Hendrix and The Chambers Brothers".

Raina: "When they weren't playing music, Seth and Gene were busy working on their Fanzines - 'Exile' and 'Cosmos' - respectively, where they were involved in every aspect of production. This endeavor allowed them to delve into the fantasy and science fiction world and was a platform for creative expression as they would write articles and contribute their own art work. I venture to guess that this sparked lifelong interests, and wonder if this spurred Gene's entrepreneurial spirit and his theatrical flair that flourished through KISS. Seth retained an interest in fantasy, horror and science fiction genres. Being

Seth's only niece, I was very close to him throughout my life, and considered him a second father. This fantasy world permeated my childhood. It's no coincidence that Halloween is my favorite holiday as I grew up with Seth's Bela Lugosi Dracula impersonations and trips to Star Trek Conventions where fans would dress in character and speak Klingon".

Pearl: "Seth was of Armenian descent. His maternal grandparents migrated to the United States to escape the Armenian genocide. Seth's father, Luther, was born in Istanbul and migrated with his family to the United States when he was around 5 years of age. Luther served in WWII and through the GI bill obtained his education, earned his master's degree in social work and became a supervisor. The opportunities and safety provided by the United States fostered a strong sense of patriotism that was passed along to Seth and to myself. Gene too shares this patriotism and has expressed his love and support for the men and women who serve and protect our country. Most people were and are still not familiar with Armenians or the genocide of the early twentieth century that occurred in Turkey where an estimated 1.5 million Armenians were exterminated. Perhaps it is this separateness from the dominant culture, a feeling of being on the outside looking in that drew Gene and Seth together on an unconscious level. There was an unspoken camaraderie of shared history, as being descendants of survivors. It is my belief that the experience of coming from a family of genocide survivors bestows certain attributes such as tenacity, ambition, and a driving work ethic. Understandably, many genocide children grow up with an awareness of the importance of conserving money and resources. It is possible that this shaped their work ethic. I recall that Gene always believed that he was destined for success and worked hard to achieve his dreams. Seth too worked hard and was the Director of Pharmacy at Coler-Goldwater Hospital at the time of his passing. Although music and art were his passion, my grandmother suggested that he opt for a more stable, known path. He devoted his focus to developing his pharmacy career, starting out with his own pharmacy store, and then working for Coler-Goldwater".

Raina: "As a baby boomer, Seth was a fan of *The Wonder Years* television series. I did not understand the allure of this program until I was older, and could appreciate the historic resonance for him. Social and political issues were coming to the forefront, Star Trek was on TV, the space program was in bloom and rock and folk music dominated the youth music scene while a revolution was gaining momentum. Seth often remarked that he had a wonderful childhood filled with great memories. He said that he grew up during a period when kids could get together and play outside, before the term "play date" became part of the lexicon, and he lamented about the loss of this time period."

Pearl: "As I look at Seth's fanzines, I am transported back to my grandparent's apartment in Jackson Heights where I can imagine two teenagers working on my grandparent's dining room table with the smell of mimeograph ink wafting through the air. Perhaps there truly was something in the air, perhaps it was synchronicity, perhaps mere coincidence, but regardless, it seemed like magical time."

Raina: "Throughout my childhood, Seth provided a constant supply of jokes, stories, and lots of music – covers of popular rock songs, and silly songs that he would invent on the spot to entertain the kids. When Karaoke was starting to become popular in NYC, we went to a local place where he received a standing ovation for *Purple People Eater*. My grandparents had a time share in the spring at the now defunct Buck Hill Inn in the Poconos that bared an eerie resemblance to the Overlook Hotel from the movie "The Shining." There were rumors of murders and paranormal activity. The rumors combined with the lack of patrons during their last few years of operation bolstered the spook factor. Seth joined us during these times where we would create amateur horror films, which included a reenactment of "The Shining" where Seth nailed Jack Nicholson's famous line with a twist *"HERE'S SETHIE*!!! " In watching

Family Jewels - Gene's funny, spur of the moment anecdotes remind me of Seth".

Pearl: "Although his professional focus was in the science area, Seth never lost his interest in art, music and science fiction. He continued to draw and paint and I recall a spare room in his first house in Huntington dedicated to his painting. I once asked about this scary carousel horse oil painting that he created, which now hangs in my home and he comically described how he was trying to capture the evilness of the carnival. Seth had a wonderful sense of humor, something that was shared by all the guys in the band."

Raina: "Seth's love and knowledge of science extended beyond his scope of practice in pharmacy as he was well versed in astronomy and physics. As a very young child, after Seth had moved out, I remember playing in his old room that he turned into an astronomer's delight by painting constellations on the ceiling surrounding by orange glowing walls. When Seth married and moved out of the city to Huntington, he purchased a telescope where he would step outside at various hours to catch whatever stars and planets were visible. Before Dr. Evil quoted "fire the laser", he helped me research and create a laser for a junior high school science project".

Raina: "Seth passed unexpectedly in 1998. Over 700 people attended his funeral services, where I had the opportunity to meet his friends and colleagues. They came from all facets of his life including an author who proclaimed Seth as his "editor" since Seth would provide him feedback about his writing, and musically inclined colleagues at the hospital that played at various hospital parties with him. Everyone wanted to tell me how they knew Seth and describe the wonderful man that he was".

Pearl: "As I finish writing this paragraph, I'm left with bitter sweet feelings. Reminiscing about someone whom I miss terribly brings back wonderful memories. I can't help but hear Captain Picard's words to "cherish each moment for it may never come again" echo in my head. I suspect that Gene and Seth's shared history of coming from families of survivors gave them an appreciation of life, fostered a philosophy of hard work, and provided them with the ability to make the most of each situation. One of my favorite quotes coined by Gene's mother, Flora "every day above ground is a good day", provides perspective when I'm down. Perhaps what rock music and KISS in particular give us is the ability to be in the moment - to live life to the fullest. Goethe urged us to "plunge boldly into the thick of life" and this is certainly how Gene and my brother Seth lived. Time waits for no one, and enjoying each moment, making the most of every opportunity is a valuable lesson that we can all incorporate into our lives."

Ross Berg

EXILE

Is published every so often (aprox. ½ly) by Seth Dogramajian at 32-66 80 St. Jackson Hts. New York N.Y. 11370... Available for Contrib, LoC, Art, Trade, or 50¢....

[illustration by Stephen Coronel]

(from the author's personal collection)

Gene Simmons

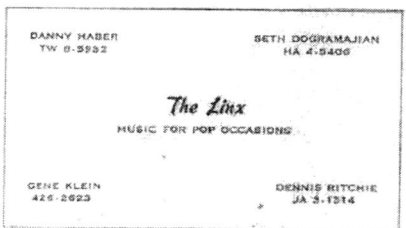

The Linx
"Music For Pop Occasions"
[Gene and Seth Business Card]
(Courtesy of the Dogramajian Family)

The Long Island Sounds
"Latest Sound in Pop Music"
[Gene and Seth Business Card]
(courtesy of the Dogramajian Family)

Ross Berg

```
Editor...
     Seth Dogramajian
     32-66 80 st. Jackson Hts.
     New York N.Y. 11370


     Deadline for next ish;
     July 4, 1969
     Material for my new Rock
     zine should be in sooner.
```

This is the March issue.........

so march! left right, left right, left...

[illustration by Gene Klein]

(from the author's personal collection)

Gene Simmons

Editorial
BRAINFOOD - Seth Dogramajian

If you received the first or second issues you will notice that my co-editor's (Danny Haber) is not here thish and will most likely not be back.

Danny and I were in the same rock band about two (maybe three) years ago. This was about the same time we put out the first <u>Exile</u> which seemed as if it was to be nought but a one shot.

Eventually the band broke up and Danny went with a group called the "Operation Blues" and Gene Klein(<u>faun</u>)and I went with a group called the "Long Island Sounds".

[illustration by Stephen Coronel]

(from the author's personal collection)

[illustration by Seth Dogramajian]

(from the author's personal collection)

Gene Simmons

FANZINE REVIEWS

by Seth Dogramajian

faun- #13 Irregular 30pgs.
exellent Ditto
Gene Klein- 33-51 84St.,Jackson Hts.
New York N.Y. 11372
Cost 25¢ or anything
Klein has broken away from his co Eds.
and his own style is allowed to
dominate the zine. He has
continued the numbers from his
old zine Cosmostilletto but has
changed the name, to protect
the innocent I guess! He rambles
a great deal and thats
good, tho many seem to dis-agree.

[illustration by Seth Dogramajian]

(from the author's personal collection)

"Growing up in an age that was a generation removed from the Holocaust, there was no true connection for a boy like me to that era. That was true until I learned about the woman behind Gene Simmons. To see a rock star speak so lovingly of his mother was unheard of. To learn why was both horrifying and inspiring. Flora survived the most evil of evil. While Gene may not have planned it, his gradual opening up about Flora's life and experiences helped put a face to the tragic events of that era. To this day, the respect and admiration Gene has for his mother serves as a reminder to us all to never forget the sins of the past and always love your mother."

-Mike Wren
Contributing Writer: KISS Magazine

"Florence is a wonderful proud mother who, after surviving such a terrible time in our modern history, created a son who is royalty in the world of Rock and Roll and beyond. Flora should be proud and I am happy to know them both in my life."

-Bruce Kulick
KISS Guitarist from 1985 to 1996

Traits and Characteristics of Children of The Holocaust:

A NEED FOR HEROES
The child sees the survivor parent as a real-life hero and object of idealization

AN ELEVATED SENSE OF IMPORTANCE
The child symbolizes the defeat of Nazism and the gift of starting anew and is often given more attention and treated with more importance than the survivor parent's spouse

DESIRE TO UNDERSTAND EVIL
The child becomes concerned with the 'dark side' in order to identify with the survivor parent's suffering

AN ACCUTE APPRECIATION OF FAMILY
The child experiences an enhanced sense of closeness to the survivor parent and feels that only family members can be truly trusted

LIVING ONE'S LIFE FOR THE DEAD
The child learns from the survivor parent that his life is to be used to make up for those whose lives were cut short and, thusly, is not to be wasted on ordinary activities

INTOLERANCE FOR WEAKNESS
The child admires the survivor parent's strength and forfeits respect for those lacking in fortitude

INTENSE MOTHER-CHILD BOND
The child is enveloped by the over-protective survivor parent who harbors inordinate fears of harm coming to the child

FEAR AND MISTRUST OF NON-JEWS
The child observes the survivor parent's cautious behavior in non-Jewish social circles and develops a deep-seated mistrust of non-Jews

CONTROL ISSUES
The child inherits the survivor parent's residual repulsion to being controlled by past oppressors

STRONG WILL TO SURVIVE
The child inherits the surviving parent's determination, ambition, resourcefulness, and fight

WORKAHOLIC
The child grows to be inordinately ambitious, motivated, successful, and hard-working so that the survivor parent's resolve to live will not have been in vain

HIGHLY PROTECTIVE OF SURVIVOR PARENT
The child, knowing that his survivor parent endured a traumatic event, will go to any length to avoid inflicting further pain upon that parent

NAMED FOR THE DEAD
The child is often named after a relative murdered in the camps in order to serve as a representative of the deceased

THE DESIRE FOR FINANCIAL SECURITY

The child observes the survivor parent's constant preparation for the next crisis and absorbs the lesson that to be financially secure is to have the ability to uproot oneself to safety at a moment's notice

A NEED TO UNDERSTAND THE UNKNOWN

The child is often unsuccessful in his efforts to learn of the survivor parent's Holocaust experiences and seeks to understand more

OUTWARD DISPLAY OF SUCCESS

The child can grow to achieve a great deal in order to compensate for the surviving parent's earlier deprivations and outwardly flaunt success in order to prove that Hitler failed

HEDONISM

The child sees the survivor parent as a victim of an indifferent universe and decides that in the end one can really only live life in a manner that makes one happy and fulfills one's specific desires; sometimes to extremes

A SENSE OF BEING SPECIAL
The child is treated by the survivor parent as a miracle of life created against insurmountable odds

FEAR AND MISTRUST OF A HOSTILE / INDIFFERENT WORLD
As a Jew and potential target of hate, the child learns from the survivor parent to present a 'mask' to the outside, non-Jewish world in order to preserve his safety

A SYMBOL OF REBIRTH
The child symbolizes a rebirth of the State of Israel and a second chance at life for the survivor parent

"My grandparents were Hungarian. When I was very young, I would often visit their apartment. They lived just a few blocks away from me. They were orthodox Jews and on every visit my Grandfather would test me on the things I learned in Yeshivah. This one day while sitting around the small kitchen table, I noticed what looked like a blue tattoo on his arm with some letters and numbers on it. 'What's that?' I asked. My grandfather looked up at me and said, 'It's because I am a Jew.' This confused me because I too was a Jew yet I did not have that on my arm. Years later, of course it became all too clear and I cried when I finally understood what had happened. We must never forget this atrocity and we must make sure, at all costs, that the world remembers. As a FREE nation, it is our duty and our responsibility to prevent this from EVER happening again--anywhere in the world. It is the duty of every free man and woman to make sure the world NEVER forgets."

-Kenny Kerner
Record Producer: "KISS" Debut Album and KISS "Hotter Than Hell"

an x-ray of his own soul

The leather-clad beast in war paint and seven-inch boot-heels advanced slowly towards the pack of wild humans at the foot of the stage. Leering at his sea of victims, the writhing gargoyle slowly craned his long neck from side to side, surveying the situation with paranoid eye balls. Gripping his instrument like an axe, the possessed ogre crept and crouched ever closer toward the teaming masses and began rolling his eyes into the back of his head until his eye sockets looked like crazed white gumballs. Pleased and deliciously encouraged at the response he received, the bat-lizard raised his brass-knuckled fist into the air and began stabbing his already beaten guitar strings into further submission - producing a tortured sound of black dissonance that filled the fetid air. Positioned to assault, the demonic creature suddenly lunged forward and a hideous stream of thick, dark blood poured furiously from his painted mouth as his giant, serpentine tongue darted hideously in and out of his bloody spout. His legs shaking spasmodically, the monster vomited the foul matter convulsively as the colony of wild-eyed spectators rushed forward to scoop the splattering overflow into their hands and onto their faces and bodies. Taking one last look at the glorious mayhem he had created, the man smiled with a mischievous twinkle in his eyes and made his exit stage right.

Later, away from the dizzying lights and punishing sounds, Gene Simmons sat alone in silence and began his ritual of wiping away the blood and the white face and the bat-shaped greasepaint and the sweat that covered his face. Working make-up remover into the creases around his eyes, he peered deeply into a small round magnified mirror and caught the reflection of a pair of eyes he had not seen in over seventeen years. They were a pair of eyes he remembered well but had not worn since he was a child staring curiously at a poster advertisement of a fat man in a red suit smoking a cigarette. The setting was New York City and a nine year old Chaim Witz had just come to America from Israel with his mother Flora. Studying the Christmas billboard closely, the young boy decided that the cheerful-looking man with his reindeer must surely be a Rabbi…and a Russian Rabbi at that, owing to the snow depicted in the illustration.

The boy looked closely. His eyes like two sponges soaking in the new sights. The new sounds and the new sights.

Eyes.

The cruel eyes of school children are upon him.

The cruel eyes of school children jeering and threatening the young boy from Israel who cannot speak English.

Gene Klein. An American name has been adapted, but still no English.

This new language sounds ugly. It is too hard to learn.
It is just too hard to learn.

Eyes.

Gazing suspiciously at his Jewish skull cap.

Eyes.

Too many eyes are upon him. Expecting too much. Expecting English. Expecting a transformation from Chaim to Gene.
Expecting a transformation.

How does the mind deal with these eyes?

When does the mind become a sanctuary from cruelty and the
non-accepting, accusing eyes?

Put on another face?
Take off another face?
Re-invent?
Hide behind?
Retreat into the mind?

Eyes.

Eyes that were now clean of make-up and sweat and blood for another night.

Eyes that now gazed upon an x-ray of his own soul – a new song. A new creation entitled "Man Of 1,000 Faces".

You don't like this face? Here's another.
You don't like that face? Here's another.
Is this face too Jewish?
Is this face more American?
Is this my real face?
Is that my real face?
What happened to my real face?

What is my real face?

A new creation.

"A Sabra is a prickly pear. It is hard on the outside with thorns; symbolic as a survival method and trait for a group of people surrounded by enemies on all sides."
- **Rabbi Brian Zacahary Mayer**

"The word Sabra comes from the name of a cactus plant that is prickly on the outside and soft and tasty on the inside. The Israeli character is often said to resemble this fruit. Why? Imagine the stress of living on the verge of constant attack; of never knowing what is going to happen tomorrow--and at the same time living, laughing, and creating. These people are UNIQUE: they are surrounded by daggers ready to slice them up, yet still find a way to enjoy life."
- **Denice Claxton**
Israel Facebook Site

sabras

The air in Haifa, Israel is thick and humid. The streets are well-traveled and while the people are hard and prickly on the outside -- they are soft and sweet on the inside. Like cactus fruit. Like a whirling twirling walking talking wandering tribe of sabras. And so they were nicknamed. And these Sabras were a restless people. Ever in motion. Ready at a moment's notice. Young Chaim watched from the hills as his people walked this way and that. Boarded this vehicle to return on another. Mathematically. Till the edges would blur. And meander. Like ants they meandered. One behind the other in lines that moved with measured purpose. Up steep hills and down narrow streets. Through fields of green and around tight corners to the bus depot where Chaim sold them the native cactus treats. The sabras were covered in spikes and Chaim would admire their jutting thorns between customer transactions; taken with the way the powerful armor served to protect the soft, vulnerable center. Taken with the possibility that spikes might someday serve to protect him as well. And he studied the sharp points. And they weaved their way into his subconscious mind. And revealed themselves as stage armor in dreams. Tomorrow, perhaps, the thorny spines would deliver him from fear.

Tomorrow, perhaps, the pointed stakes would shield him from the crowd they drew.

Today, for now, the boy's protection arrived in the shape of a song.

Like a nervous mumble or muttering of white noise designed to distract the listener from hearing the colors of his deepest fears. A lilting drone to take the place of awkward silence and intrusion of thought. A melody of the young author's personal making; with apologies, to be sure, to the regional minor scales that informed him.

Young Chaim watched from the hills as his people walked this way and that.

And as that plane touched down at Laguardia, he reached up to hold his mother's hand. The air in Flushing, Queens was thick and humid. The streets were well-traveled and while the people outside seemed hard and prickly, Uncle Larry and Aunt Magda were soft and sweet as they welcomed Chaim and his mother Flora inside. Inside; where young Chaim discovered a large television set and a ringing telephone and a humming refrigerator and cold bottles of soda pop and thick containers of tangy ketchup and spongy loaves of cellophane-wrapped white bread and large square windows framing an outer world of grocery stores and speeding cars and racing bikes and traffic lights. As a hot, crackling picture tube powered the screen's flickering images - - Chaim's eyes feasted on 'Planet Patrol' and 'Superman'. Pursing his lips and clenching his teeth and pressing his tongue to the roof of his mouth, Chaim practiced and mimicked the sounds of America.

From his bedroom window, he watched the people and cars and buses and bicycles;
ever in motion.
This way.
That way.
Edges.
Blurred.
Ants.
Meandering.
Measured.
Purpose.
Steep.
 Hills.
Tight.
Corners.

It was so like Haifa. Even the hot dog vendors made him dream of his sabra stand.

It was so like America. The whirling twirling shake and shifting fevered enormity of sights and sounds and tastes and smells and sweet and soft and hard and prickly.

Sometimes the enormity washed over him in waves of excitement and wonder at what the future might hold. Sometimes its vastness left him lost in uncertainty. Some nights he took to the edge of his mattress, to summon his armor, as if as in prayer. And rocking his body in fixed, gentle intervals -- eyes closed, knees to his chest -- he listened to a soft lilting drone. A melody of his personal making. With apologies, to be sure, to the regional minor scales of a life left behind.

"The natural, maternal instinct amplifies and increases by the THOUSANDS when your child is in danger. There is not another feeling like it in the world and there are no words that can describe it. It is a spiritual connection with your child that physically pulls you by your heart and is all-consuming."
-Carla Fink
Music Industry Artist Consultant and Producer/Recording/Studio Referral Service

"A mother's heart is always with her children!"
-Danni Bee
Member: The Flora Army

what was once a banana stalk

Like a witch flanking a bubbling cauldron, he set about concocting the ingredients of his stage blood. He had seen rivers of blood as a child and knew that it was thick and that it glistened. He remembered it reminded him of maple syrup and so he added it to the egg mucous and to the milk-curdled custard and to the lumpy pellets of cottage cheese that served to simulate the globs of vessel chunks that had spattered onto his face that terrible day. It was the recipe to the crimson red bloodbath that still haunted his dreams. Only this time, he would control when and how the blood would flow. And flow it did. As did the memories of his past.

Climbing that fig tree was difficult work, but a chance at impressing the others made it worth the effort. As he triumphantly reached the top branch, little Chaim looked down to notice the children scrambling in all directions at the sound of the woman's shrill voice. Too many times these children – these neighborhood pests, these crop-destroying locusts, had scaled her tree and murdered her branches and ravished her figs and scattered through the streets and into the shadows like the pack of rats that they were. As always, they had gotten away. They had all escaped. All but one. And so clutching the banana stalk, tightening and then loosening her grip in anticipation, she watched and she waited as the small boy made his way back down the trunk of the tree. After many minutes of strategic descent, his two feet finally met the ground where her weapon struck him sharply in the gut. Struggling for balance, he was knocked to the ground with a blow to his left shoulder. Terrified and running towards home he screamed in agony as he was hammered a final time in the back of the leg.

Arriving into the safety of his mother's arms, she wiped his tears and sought answers. "Who did this to you?" "Why did it happen?" "Did you cause the trouble?"

Holding hands, mother and child marched back to the house that bathed in the shadow of the large fig tree.

The door opened.

"Did you hit my child?"

"Yes, I did."

"Can you tell me what you hit my child with?"

"I hit him with this. I gave him a thrashing. No one climbs my tree." The proclamation concluded with a smirk.

Flora lurched forward and wrestled the banana stalk from the woman with both hands. Chaim's eyes widened as he watched his mother club the woman atop the head and back. The blood was everywhere. And it turned the banana stalk into a Staff of Justice. A Staff of Righteousness.
Yesterday, they hurt her family.
Today, they would not.
Last time, she was a frightened girl.
This time she was a mother.
And no one hurts my boy. No one touches my son. No one. Ever.

She repeated these words to the Sergeant who looked to his officers for ideas and received not a one. Finally, he ventured, "But you can't just walk about striking people…"
"She hit my son."
"I know, but you can't just…"
"No one hits my child."
"I realize that you…"
"No one hits my child, Sergeant, and if *you* ever touch him I'll knock you over the head, too."
This remark filled the room with nervous titters, but Flora wasn't laughing. The Sergeant - taken aback - looked side to side at his deputies, shrugged his shoulders, and smiled: "Take your son and go home."

Holding hands, mother and child walked together from the station in the cool breeze of the evening to their home.

"Mother, I hurt. My stomach and legs. They hurt."

"I know, my beautiful son. But you will get better. You are alive and that is all that matters. You are alive, Chaim."

He looked up at her face and smiled at the way the moon's glow shimmered and reflected in her dark eyes.

Smiling back at him, she added: "Remember, my son - any day above ground is a good day."

And arriving home, Chaim curled up in his mother's lap; secure once more in her arms. Secure once more in her reassuring smile.

"Is Gene Simmons the man he is today because of the man his father wasn't?"

-Norman Huizenga
Co-Founder: The KISS Detention Hall

"In October of 1975, KISS came and played Cadillac High School where my father was a teacher. I was only around 5 or 6 years old. Gene was really sweet and was posing for pictures with a lot of the little kids. He seemed to have a 'fatherly' nature. He wanted to me to sit on his lap for a photo but I wouldn't because I was afraid of all of the spikes on his costume."

-Sean Williams
KISS In Cadillac 1975 Facebook Page

"The story of Flora Klein and her only son is one of heartache, perseverance, and triumph. It is by no means a happy story, but one that needs telling again and again so that the world may never forget."

-Klown: KISS Tribute Band

enormously much and overwhelmingly little

What they shared in common was both enormously much and overwhelmingly little. Flora and Yechiel met and married after the liberation of the camps; the numbers on their arms uniting them in a shared experience of survival. A joyous event soon followed their union, yet Yechiel was absent the day his only son entered the world. As the young boy grew, Chaim came to understand that his father - a fine sculptor of wood with a talent as great as his deficits for business - was frequently away from the home in search of work. This lonely routine went on for years with Flora listening often as Yechiel described the emptiness that accompanied his separation from wife and child. And so it was with loving anticipation that Flora set out with her son that day to find Yechiel - - to lift his spirits with a gift of family unexpected. Searching the town for a sign of Yechiel, Mother and child smiled at one another with a shared excitement. As day turned into early evening, they found themselves in the large, ornate lobby of a local cinema. Chaim's eyes began to study and follow the elaborate swirling patterned lines of the crimson red wallpaper as it curved around an adjacent wall and up a narrow staircase. Craning his neck to determine whether the patterned paper continued up the flight of stairs, Chaim peered upwards and saw his father. His excitement was immediately replaced by confusion: "Mother, who is that blonde woman kissing Papa?" Turning quickly, Flora gasped - - her face distorted in pain. They fled to the train station in stunned silence.

He leaned in and studied the Psychiatrist's eyes: "My father did not *leave* us.
My father *abandoned* us.
He failed as a person by abandoning his child. By abandoning my mother.

And we were left with nothing.
So she worked two jobs. And the screams that awoke me from my terrible dreams went untreated. No one was there. She was working. My fears turned into rage. My safety was gone. No one was there to hold me anymore. Not when I awoke from my nightmares."

There was no money. There was no Father. There was no Husband. But there was a son. And the son could take the place in many ways. And so he did. And so he set about collecting his weekly delivery monies that cold Winter morning. The door opened and the stench of alcohol on the lady's breath caused the teenaged Chaim to take two steps in reverse.

He was invited inside.
Backward steps
became
forward steps.
He was instructed to sit on the couch.
And froze as she mounted him.

When it was over, young Chaim escaped from the house and the woman and her couch and her alcohol breath and he prayed to God he hadn't broken any laws.

And that was the first time.

Women.

My God, there had been *thousands*. Every size and every shape and every culture and every religion. Thousands of times over. The Roadie was skeptical, but Gene was more than eager to prove his claim. The large book was presented as a great trophy - - a heavy black scrapbook filled with Polaroid photographs of female conquests.....arranged with care like a book of pinned butterflies. Pinned specimens gathered and displayed in assorted poses.

As the discussion ended and his employee closed the door behind him, Gene dimmed the last remaining light in his hotel room. "Control life or it controls you", Gene said, shifting his gaze toward nothing in particular.

"As a species, we can learn from our ancestors and especially from those who have survived the Holocaust. This was a time in history when Mankind turned on one another instead of embracing different cultures and backgrounds. We believe music has a strong impact on bringing people together and it should be celebrated often."

-Anthony Miller
'Almost Human' KISS Tribute Band

"My Great-Grandmother fled Hungary to the United States but her brother wasn't so lucky. He was sent to a concentration camp and his job was to clean out the gas chambers. One day, he found his wife and children in the gas chamber and was forced to remove their bodies and bury them together in a mass grave with the other dead bodies."

-Audrey Tobi Jones Baker
Member: The Flora Army

sweet serenading silence

The mimeograph flyer read:
SEE THE LONG ISLAND SOUNDS
GENE, STEVE, SETH, ALLEN, AND STAN
AT THE JEWISH CENTER
OF JACKSON HEIGHTS
82ND STREET AND 34 AVENUE
MAY 27, 1966

Arriving at the small recreation room within the larger facility, the five high school bandmates went about rearranging the room and setting up their equipment. Clusters of neighborhood kids and retired folk alike dotted the room as they passed the time playing cards and checkers and hangman and backgammon. Mostly the old folks liked to gather together and talk. With special care, Gene removed his new bass guitar from its case. A Japanese copy in the Hofner style made famous by The Beatles. It was purchased for $35 with love and a lot of hard work by Flora for her son. She couldn't particularly afford it, but felt it was important to support Gene's burgeoning interest in music. Stan positioned his floor tom and twisted the drum key on his snare. Resting on his swivel chair he surveyed his kit and smiled. He smiled because he knew this was what he wanted to do. He had his whole life ahead of him. And his used set had a silver finish he was especially proud of. Seth sat on the floor and stretched out a microphone cord, attaching electrical tape where necessary to the well-worn appliance as Allen and Stephen hunted for wall plugs to accommodate the band's growing collection of battered amplifiers and speaker cases.

Alone at the back of the room sat Vladek, pretending not to care or to notice the teens. He buried his head in the newspaper headlines and didn't want to know about any musicians, that was for sure. A frail gentleman appearing older than his 53 years, Vladek wore a premature scowl in anticipation of the coming noise. He did not want to hear music. Not anymore. Not after what they did to it. How they perverted it and turned the melodies of God into the maladies of Satan. How they forced him to use his trumpet like a Pied Piper; lulling the new arrivals into a sense of false safety. Playing as the healthy were separated from the sick.

Performing sweet couplets as executions were ordered.

Fingering playful waltzes as prisoners hung lifeless from gallows.

Serenading softly as women and children were marched unwittingly to the gas chambers.

Life-affirming, beautiful music rang out as they marched.

They played all night as the Nazis counted the live ones and the dead ones. The whole night sometimes they stood and they played. The count went on again and again to the measured sound of the orchestra's meter. When those in line could no longer stand straight, their necks were snapped on planks of wood. All the while, Vladek's trumpet sang "All Vogel Sind Schon Da" into the cool night air.

"Testing, testing….one….two….three", Seth spoke into the PA System; his bandmates laughing at the requisite squeal of microphone feedback.

But *mostly*, Vladek remembered……*mostly* the SS wanted music for their working. For their pleasure. It helped them to their jobs enjoy. Dr. Mengele, especially. The trains with human cargo would arrive with the orchestra playing "J'attendrai Ton Retour". Enraptured so by the music, Dr. Mengele would smile and sway and would this way and that way like a musical Conductor float. Like a Conductor waves his baton this way for life and this way for death. Like a man conducting in sheer bliss an orchestra on a cloud:

You to live. You to die.

Music from heaven's glorious bosom. Sheer bliss.

Wielder of the baton.

A hi-hat snapped and a bass line walked and a handsome youngster smiled as he gripped the microphone stand. "Hi, I'm Seth Dogramajian and we're 'The Long Island Sounds'. Hopefully you're in the mood for some music today….." Vladek wasn't. He never again would be. So he pushed his paper aside and left the building. In search of silence.

"If creativity is a form of exorcism, the art and accomplishments of Gene Simmons are a lifelong triumph over the evil that once threatened his family and his people."

-Stephen Lord
Founder: Crime Writers of South Australia

"Gene Simmons has a fantastic American Dream story based on his Jewish principals and ethics learned from his Mom."

- Gordon G.G. Gebert
Author: "KISS & Tell"

"Flora must be a very proud Mother - and I am thankful for her for giving me one of my Favorite Rock Stars of all time: Gene Simmons."

-Farrow Customs
Custom Design KISS Action Figures

is there room for three?

To be an only child.
To be an only child of a mother who survived the murderous intentions of Adolph Hitler.
To be an only child of a mother who survived an unfaithful and abandoning husband.
To be an only child of a mother who looked to her one son to serve as the flower that survives, thrives, and blooms in defiance of the evil that tried, and failed, to extinguish life.

The only child.
The only child who has no built-in peers.
The only child who learns not how to socialize with others his age.
The only child who is searching for a brother.

Searching for the brother he was never given by mother...

Nineteen Sixty-One.
Gene Klein spends his days with Stephen Coronel.
Talking,
Laughing,
Sharing,
Drawing,
Writing,
Creating works of fiction and fantasy.

Nineteen Sixty-Six.
Gene and Stephen play guitar together. Gene and Stephen write
songs together. Gene and Stephen write and illustrate fanzines
together. Gene and Stephen chase skirts together.

Gene and Stephen.
Nineteen Sixty-Nine.
Stephen Coronel and Stanley Eisen. Guitars in hand. Jamming. Playing. Sharing a feeling and an afternoon.

Enter Gene Klein.

Stanley this is Gene. Gene this is Stanley. Stanley writes songs too.

Nineteen Seventy.
Gene Klein. Stephen Coronel. Brothers.

Nineteen Seventy-One.
Gene Klein. Stephen Coronel. Stanley Eisen. Brothers?
Is there room for three?

"You're playing the guitar lead too fast again, Stephen!"

"Screw off, Stan! You think you've got some special aura around you or something? You think you're such an expert?"

And three becomes a crowd.

Nineteen Seventy-Two.
Epic records comes-a-calling with money, promises, and legal contracts in hand………….on condition: replace Stephen Coronel.
Replace Stephen? Can you just replace a brother?

"Replace the funny looking guy with the weird curly hair and you've got your record deal."

But what if the funny looking guy with the weird curly hair is your best friend? What if he is the brother you never had? The one you talked with
laughed with
shared with
dreamed with…..

He was there with you when you were a child.

When you were a child.

When you were a child your mother Flora told you that you were better than the other children. Your mother Flora told you that you were the most special of all of the children. Your mother Flora told you that your very existence was a miracle. Your mother Flora is a survivor. She survived. If she could survive the camps then you, Gene Klein, can certainly survive anything. You can succeed in the face of any challenge…..in the face of any obstacle. You can succeed – but will you choose to? Did Flora survive the camps for you to add up to nothing or did she survive the camps so that you could set the world ablaze with your dreams and ambitions and passions to succeed beyond anyone's wildest imaginings? What will you allow to stand between you and your dreams in this life? You were always the most special of all of the children.

Gene signed the contract.

And was once again an only child.

"The best way to take the sting out of an affront is to embrace it as your own and deflate the power it formerly had."

Oscar Cargas
Member: The Flora Army

"I live with the pain of not having a family everyday. I never had an Aunt or an Uncle or brothers or grandparents. They all perished in the war. I was born in Poland and being a Jew at that time was certain death. Hell, I don't even have the date and time of my birth. I was born right there in the middle of it. I was brought up by parents who were so tortured by the memories, they could not live in the moments of bringing myself and my sister up with joy. Never Forget? Hell no...I can't."

-Genya Ravan
Punk Rock Pioneer/Holocaust Survivor

"How can we "forget" a situation that almost annihilated our people? It has been, is, and should ALWAYS be, in the forefront of our consciousness."

-Richard "Handsome Dick" Manitoba
Lead Singer/The Dictators

all relative

For every creature that experiences the excruciating agony of being devoured alive is another experiencing the ecstasies of dominance and satiation. For every child who learns of the torment and dehumanization of his ancestors is another regaled by swashbuckling tales of his forefathers; tales of promise and power and prosperity and pride. Tales of a romantic era sadly in the past where music was sweeter and food was the best it had ever tasted.

These were the golden years.

The best of times.

The good old days.

And so the man's time as a soldier during World War II was described to his young relative – many years before the boy would learn to play guitar or change his name to Ace. To the young Frehley, it was all presented in a rather cartoonish manner – divorced from the horrors of the death camps – the older man described the glamour of it all: The War Merit Crosses and General Assault Badges. The M35 helmets with riveted air vents and rolled rims. The black leather three-quarter length Jackboots with steel toes and hob-nailed soles. The silver shoulder boards and rank collar patches. And, perhaps most fetching to the young boy's eyes: the lightning bolt SS Nazi unit insignia. Far more than the Schutzstaffel Death's Head emblem, the lightning bolt symbol fired the child's imagination with a riveting sense of power

and destiny. It was a design he would summon some fifteen years later whilst setting about crafting a logo. For a band.
He had just joined.

Frehley seized a pencil, a ruler, and a can of beer and worked into the night.

Upon viewing the proposed SS design, Simmons' hand balled into a fist. His mind latched onto an image of an impeccably dressed German SS Officer breaking gold teeth out of the jaws of the dead - the Officer never losing his air of cultured sophistication as he pulled wedding rings from lifeless fingers or cut hair to the scalp to be used for mattresses and rope. Corpses were carted in tubs to incineration rooms while trousers kept their perfect creases. Smoldering bodies were stirred with steel hooks while boots kept a pristine shine. Unburned bones were smashed to dust and sold as human bone-meal to fertilizer companies; all the while, crisp armbands adorned with the Nazi swastika decorated the uniforms of dapper and refined members of the Master Race. Never was a hair out of place or a bead of sweat impolitely displayed. The Nazis and their symbols were the ultimate declarations of perfection, nobility, and regal seriousness. These were things that Gene had read. These were things he knew.

Simmons was so filled with rage he thought he would be sick.

He leaned in - and suddenly found himself, for no particular reason, struggling to make out the three words written on Frehley's t-shirt. Looking Ace straight in the eye, Gene opened his mouth to speak but, distracted, stopped. Frehley let out a nervous cackle and then flinched as Simmons moved towards him again. Snapping and popping like a fried egg, the synapses in Gene's brain were firing in all directions. Should he belt this guy? Should he fire him? Should he belt him and *then* fire him? And then belt him again? In the midst of these questions, he couldn't help but glance down at the guitarist's shirt once more, squinting in an attempt to decipher the code:

MAX'S KANSAS CITY

And there it stood. On Park Avenue South. Between 17th Street and 18th Street in New York City. Max's Kansas City. With a nightclub up top and a restaurant down below. Max's. "Steak, Lobster, Chick Peas". And Jews. Lots of Jewish kids. Playing up top and answering to names like Blum and Weinstein and Hyman and Mizrahi. Kids whose folks had survived the camps. Kids who now gathered together to make degenerate art. Degenerate Jewish art. Kids who shouldn't even be alive creating what Hitler deemed to be degenerate.

So alive.

So very alive the way they played. So alive - playing up top while the Fuhrer resided down below. And they played their degenerate music but they did something more. They took Adolph's beloved symbols of majestic seriousness and they made them foolish and they made them camp. Goose-stepping idiotically around the stage like a pack of Colonel Klinks, the audiences and the performers alike howled gleefully at the failed seriousness of the Nazis and their symbols and affectations.

And away from the stage, the mocking and defiling of these symbols intensified.

Grueling sessions of potent animal-like fornication atop Nazi flags yielded the oppressive symbols thoroughly impotent as they were left soaked in vile bodily secretions and oozing fish-scented discharge. Sweaty testicles flapped and flopped ridiculously over every inch of the flag while semen-soaked pubic hairs detached, settled and crusted onto the fabric like hardened boogers. Cakes of dried period blood flakes dislodged and embedded into the stitchery while glistening rectal holes dripped a salty gruel that seeped deep within the swastika design. Engaging in sublime pleasure atop the symbol of what was supposed to have killed them was not lost on the participants and made the proceedings all the more delicious.

Revenge incarnate. That's what was playing out in and around Max's. Kids playing rock and roll and dancing on Hitler's grave. These were things that Gene had read. These were things he knew.

And shifting his gaze back towards the guitarist,

Simmons paused to think a moment longer.

He imagined a time - not so far from now - when he too, a survivor of a survivor - with guitar in hand, would make degenerate Jewish art beneath the blinding light of a thousand glowing bulbs in the shape of the lightning bolt SS's; he, a boy from Israel, darting his nasty tongue in and out lasciviously - awash in the illumination of Hitler's symbol of refined culture - and mocking it. Mocking and defiling it with legs that shake spastically as a projectile blood discharge violently bursts and then dribbles down his chin like putrid asshole sweat soiling a Nazi flag.

Gene smiled at the image. He lowered his fist into a handshake and it was over. The failed symbol of the Final Solution would do just fine. In fact, it would be a real hoot for a Jewish kid who never should have been born to claim it as his own, pervert its original meaning, and wind up with more women, power, fame, money, and happiness than any man could ever dream of. Stranger things had happened. After all, this was America. And he was a kid with ideas.

"Throughout Jewish history - from Samson to modern Jews who still adhere to Orthodox laws dictating the cutting and wearing of hair - power and sensuality have always been represented by hair."
-Rabbi Samuel Levin

"The Jewish people's deliverance from Hitler was the first day of building an Israeli State. Long life to Israel!"
-Jean-Maurice Monier
Member: The Flora Army

"When I was 19, I met an elderly woman who was - to my surprise - a Holocaust survivor. It only took a slight slip of her 3/4 length chiffon shirt and a peak of her forearm to cause me to gasp in horror. There - staring back at me - was her serial number tattoo. As my eyes remained locked on her arm, all I could say uncontrollably was 'I'm sorry.' As tears welled in both our eyes."
-Ashley Bueche
Author/Poet

by it's very nature

Away from the stage, in a quieter place in a future space - a mirror's reflection informed the beast that his thick, shiny waves of golden brown hair had now extended from the top of his skull clear down to the bottom of his unusually long face; his lustrous curls empowering him with the strength and confidence of the biblical Samson. With a spiked knuckled fist, the creature gathered the tangle of hair and yanked and affixed it to the summit of his head in a wild top knot crest - forcing the remainder of his hair to stream out from his crown in a three-way frizz befitting a demonic circus clown. The beast thought he looked very much like an ancient Barbarian. And he liked it.

That hair.

He found himself smiling and nodding at the sight of it. Yes, that would do just fine. He watched the Jewish prisoner complete one final pincurl and dismissed her like a dog with the wave of a hand.

For Flora Klein - every hair roll, fingerwave, do-rag, back curl, rag curl, vertical wave, net-tie, page-boy, coil tail, dip low, ribboning procedure performed on the officer's wife's hair was a literal stay of execution.

>*the flowing glowing golden hair*
>*belonging to commandant's wife*
>*did constant care require there*
>*and thusly saved the young Jew's life*

Die Fahigkeiten des Gafangenen wurden identifiziert und als nutzlich fur unsere Operation bewertet. Notiere die folgenden Wahrheiten da sie zur Ausbildung gehoren.

(TRANSLATION: The prisoner's skills have been identified and deemed valuable to the whole of our operation. Note the following truths as they relate to training)

"By it's very nature it will resist all efforts to be altered in any way. As such, every strand must be saturated to the core to allow for easy manipulation and transformation. It is not sufficient to merely coat the surface; the very essence of it must be tamed and controlled. Throughout the entire procedure it is necessary to maintain total influence; if not, it will only be partially softened and, thus, unwilling to accept it's new form. Because the goal is to manipulate the very roots, it is often necessary to exert a certain measure of pressure and force; though this may lead to permanent damage. Regular treatments will be necessary to control and ultimately obliterate it's natural tendency to create waves."

Touching her bald head, Flora's mind disassociated and dissolved into fragments of her past. Where her long hair once served as a beautiful, glowing marker of her health, strength, fidelity, and fertility - her shaven, scaly pate now only communicated the loss of her personal power and beauty.

Could it ever return?
In a future space, perhaps.
In a future space where
the strong lift up
the weak.

Where the free
liberate
the enslaved.
Where a terrible evil is defeated and a Jewish
State rises from the ashes.
Maybe then.
God, let it be true.

"There have been many insane events that have occurred throughout the course of history on this planet, and the Holocaust is certainly one of the most horrific! I feel that remembering the Holocaust gives good reason to recognize the evils that exist in our world today, and to support any war that defeats them!"

-Richie Fontana
Drummer on KISS "Dynasty" album and "Paul Stanley" 1978 Solo Album

"What can you say about Florence Klein? So few survived the Holocaust. She is the Heart and Soul of Gene Simmons! To know the story of Florence Klein and Chaim Witz is to know the story of two very special people!"

-Cynthia Nash Sebring
Member: KISS Army Florida

"Even a rock star as titanic as Gene Simmons can't escape his family's roots in the Holocaust. To his everlasting credit, he does not sweep it aside or try to forget it."

-Joel Selvin
Music Critic/Rock Journalist

of delicate hands and bodies burning

And as the painted fiend drew the flaming torch in for a second successive shower of exploding kerosene-laced saliva on that sweat-soaked stage in that delapitated hotel in those final hours in that year 1973, a halo of fire surrounded the beast's jutting matted clown hair and began eating through the pocked valleys of his melting scalp. Glowing like the hot embers of a burning charcoal fire, the nodules on his skull seared and swelled and liquefied into a flaming lump of burning hair and gristled brain matter.

Gene Simmons was on fire.

The smoke was black and thick.

And everything and everyone was engulfed in flames.

And into the fire went people.

Women.

Children.

Babies.

An SS officer cooked a potato over the fire that engulfed the heap of bodies.

Flora closed her eyes but she still could not sleep. Even all these years later, it was sometimes hard to sleep.

On this particular night, the flames were very vivid and clear in Flora's senses. She remembered, as if it were yesterday, being 14 years old and watching her mother walk her own mother into the gas chamber, not wanting the old woman to face death alone.

Flora longed for her mother. Sometimes she struggled to remember what her mother had looked like. Other times, Flora could see her mother's hands, smell her mother's hair and hear her soft knowing laugh without even trying.

This was one such night; for each time she closed her eyes she saw her mother's delicate hands and smelled the bodies in the fire.

Abruptly scrambling the sights and smells of her past, a knock at the door.

Flora shuddered.

A small piece of her always knew they would return.

The Germans. Dragging Jews out of their homes and beating them in the streets and laughing as they soiled themselves from fear in front of their children.

And now they had found her. With a knock at the door, another Jew to drag into the street and squeeze into a cattle car and toss into an oven like they should have the last time they missed their chance.

Another knock and the door moved; not to reveal a German officer but her beloved son, Chaim. He saw the look in her eyes and knew the evening had been filled with fire.

Chaim Klein was acutely aware that the most important and defining event of his life had occurred before he was even born. The mantra 'Never Forget' had been burned into his brain despite the fact that he could not remember a thing. He did not know what it was to survive a Nazi concentration camp. He did not know the true pain of starvation or the threat of death at any moment. He only knew that the other children's parents did not have numbers on their arms. He only knew that while other children's parents loved them, they did not gaze upon them like genuine miracles in the flesh. He only knew that the other children's parents had parents. He only knew how little he knew.

Embracing his mother, he returned to his bedroom and scrawled into his journal of future song titles: "My Mother Is The Most Beautiful Woman In The World".

That much he knew.

And as Chaim slept and dreamt of gliding triumphantly above the New York skyline stamping out evil wherever it grew, Flora dreamed of fire. Fire that transforms radiant beautiful life into inanimate dust. Fire that destroys the evidence.

When the flames were at last extinguished, the gargoyle rose to his feet and spread his batwings victoriously before his dazed flock of tattered worshippers.

Fire be damned.

Flora lived to create a child called 'Life' and he was the tangible proof of her survival; the ultimate defeat of Nazism.

The holiest of water had quenched the fire and the survivors had created life.

Hitler lost.

"I met Flora Klein at The New York Official KISS Convention - I was performing there as the drummer for KISS Tribute band 'ALIVE'. She is a very nice lady...was well dressed, held her head high, good posture. Sat with her back straight legs crossed. Very "regal" looking, I remember thinking. Very friendly and nice-talkative, but not overly. Struck me as very confident, but not arrogant. You can see where Gene gets his confidence from...

It was at the Roseland Ballroom. There is a side-door off stage just by the stairs to the dressing rooms. We were mingling on-stage prior to the doors being open and she walked in this side-door. I recognized her from pics in magazines. When she waked on stage, I noticed she was unescorted, I introduced myself and I asked her if she would like me to have someone let Gene know she was there-she said "No, darlink...I dont vant to botha him, he is VORKING." She had a very cute Hungarian accent. So I asked if she wanted a chair, and got her one. We made small talk.
When we were playing, Flora watched the show-and when Spiro (Gene in 'ALIVE') looked over at her, Flora stuck out her tongue, and did the "devil horns" hand sign!"

-Archie Gamble
Drummer: KISS Tribute band 'ALIVE'

full

"One day, and I assure you it will be soon", leered the beast, "I shall *well* know the taste of human flesh." The reporter paused to digest the words he thought he had just heard. Smiling uneasily, he studied the figure before him; looking closer now at his subject's insect jewelry, black nail polish, and seven-inch platform boots.

After a terrifying experience of finding a giant spider in his yarmulke as a child, Gene had long since taken to decorating his body with spider rings, bracelets, and necklaces in a conscious attempt to overcome his fear of the black sinister creepy creatures. Onstage, he performed before a great spiderweb backdrop -- effectively becoming the very spider that once paralyzed him with fear; effectively flirting with the macabre in an effort to understand and control the evil that still so affected his mother and therefore himself. Menacingly, the creature abandoned his chair and approached the writer within two inches of his face. Shifting his eyes uncomfortably, the reporter cleared his throat self-consciously and fumbled with his notes. Helpless to keep his subject's hot breath from penetrating his skin, the writer lifted his head to find himself staring directly and unexpectedly into a large gaping oral cavity. He could only wince and recoil as his host proceeded to roll his eyes deep into the back of his head. Unsettled, the man scrambled for his note pad and scanned the room for an escape route.

"I imagine it to be quite tender and fortifying. Human flesh, I mean."

The creature then revealed his serpentine tongue and rolled it slowly across the front of his teeth; the journalist watching now as the knob to the front door began moving slowly from left to right. The writer jumped and clutched his chest as the door suddenly sprang open and slammed into the adjacent wall: revealing a small woman carrying several grocery bags.

"Chaim! My darling son!"

The reporter turned quickly towards Gene who began to blush at the sound of his birthname revealed. "Have you and your handsome friend eaten lunch yet? Well, I'll just make you two hungry boys some matzo ball soup."

Gene glanced at the writer with an impish grin while the man, feeling had, grabbed his coat and exited Gene's apartment in a huff. Gene took some minutes to flatten his hair down and shed his macabre jewelry.

"Here is your soup, my darling son! Where is your friend? He left without eating? He looked like such a hungry boy."

And with that, mother and son sat at a small kitchen table and ate matzo ball soup; their sentences traveling in and out of Hungarian, English, and Hebrew as they kibbitzed together. Long into the early evening.

"Behind every life story is a ghost story. Some never face these phantoms, or understand the forces that shaped them. Others find a way to coexist. And, in the most triumphant of narratives, the ghosts are not only conquered, but transformed into a source of power."

-Keith Elliot Greenberg
Author: "December 8, 1980:
The Day John Lennon Died"

"I spent the day with Gene at a Toledo rock station back in 1975. He was very mild-mannered as he took phone calls and gave away copies of the KISS "Alive!" record. At the conclusion of the promotional venture, Gene got ready for the evening's show and emerged from his room as **Godzilla**! The transformation was *very* real and *quite* astounding."

-John Rockwood
KISS Photographer

"The golem creation has been a facet of folklore for centuries. Nothing is more fascinating than a creature being born not as a result of an accident, but of the willful desire of the self. The man-made monster."

-Robert Gomez
Comic Book Enthusiast

dust and clay

The slave can become the master. This is a known fact. Ask any man who has created a Golem and, if he is truthful, he will tell you as much. A Golem is a dangerous creature. One to be both feared and admired. It is a reckless figure known to potentially harm its creator; growing in strength over time as it does. Yet historically, for the Jewish people, the returns have always warranted the risks. This was certainly true for 16th century Rabbi Judah Lowe who created the Golem of Prague as a means to uncover plots against the Jews and to punish anti-semitic perpetrators. At Yeshiva, young Chaim studied the endeavors of Rabbi Lowe and dreamed of the day he too would become a Rabbi; smiling at the thought of mesmerizing a rapt congregation with his actions and his words. Chaim learned that just as God had created Adam from dust and clay, so too had men throughout history - in an effort to gain some of God's wisdom and power - sought to create life from dust and clay. As the young boy came to discover more and more horrifying truths about the Nazi death camps, his imagination became narrowly focused on a single fantastical wish: to have somehow created a Golem that would have protected and saved his mother's family from Adolph Hitler. Sometimes his fantasy revolved around *creating* the Golem and other times his imaginings centered around *becoming* the Golem itself; either way, the dream always had the same ending: the man-made superhero would rescue the Jews in peril by destroying the anti-semitic threat and - when that mission was accomplished - the Golem would revert back to the clay and sandlike particles from which it had been created.

As childhood gave way to adolescence, Chaim became Gene and Gene became infatuated with monsters. Some, like Frankenstein's creation, were Golems produced by specific ambitious men. Others, like the Phantom of the Opera, were monsters created by society. Creatures such as Godzilla and King Kong were exploited and manipulated by Man until they sought vengeance upon the human race; finally cracking under the weight of sheer antagonism. These monsters were often misunderstood. They were the 'other'. Outside of society. Some were from other worlds; from other countries - as Gene was. And so the young man cried when Kong fell to his death from the skyline above. He buried his head in his hands as the villagers destroyed Frankenstein's Golem with their fiery torches - the creature unable to speak the language and explain his innocence. The creature and Gene alike. Unable to speak the language.

The creature and Gene alike.
Powerless.
Unable to speak.
Apart from.
Other.

Monsters. They consumed his every thought. Some of them were victimized and misunderstood. Like Gorgo. And Reptilicus. Some of them were victim*izers* that Gene could *never* understand. Like Hitler. Monsters. There was a growing need. A compulsion. To view macabre films. To read fantasy magazines. To create horror fanzines. To ask questions about the Holocaust.

The young man began to harvest fragments. To build the ingredients for a Golem. The pieces were all there. And in they went. Thick abscessed chunks. As if into a bubbling stew. As if into a simmering cauldron. One by one they were weighed and considered; each one affixing itself to the larger coagulated mass. The final ingredient was the shadow flash that fell upon the disfigured pig face of Lon Chaney's 'Phantom'; forming a bat-shaped pattern design that burned itself into Gene's memory forever.

Preparing the 4 inch die cut textured sponge from a block wedge, Gene steadied the circular compact of Kaolinite Clay and dipped his latex instrument of application into the layered silicate minerals; attaching the clay to the dry powdered foundation dust and marrying the two properties as God and Rabbi Lowe had done so ably before him.

The young man from the holy land of Israel had hatched a Golem. An alter-ego. A life-form created from dust and clay and dreams and nightmares. A Golem who would take it's maker to places he never could have gone; to heights he never would have scaled. A Golem who would grow to be as iconic as Mickey Mouse and as powerful as Superman. A Golem who would captivate the youth of the world and heroically defend the Jewish people against religious zealots and fringe groups throughout the land. And, as is always the risk, a Golem who often could not be controlled by it's creator: on the occasions it would terrorize and drench it's underlings in spit from the sides of the stage, the Golem would be deactivated and returned to the elements from which it had been created. To the blackened finger-smeared jars of clay and chipped tattered compacts of dust powder. Laying in wait to be infused with life again.

"I used to love to grab my camera and point it real quick at Gene when he wasn't wearing his KISS make-up. He would try to frantically hide his face with a napkin or a hat. But I was just joking and Gene and I would laugh about it afterwards."

-Richard E. Aaron
KISS Photographer

"When most people think of Gene Simmons - the image of a legendary, face painted, larger-than-life rock star is what comes to mind. Few people stop to think about the tremendous perseverance and belief in oneself it takes to attain that level of success. Fewer still consider where Gene got those qualities. The strength his mother, Flora – and her ability to survive the Holocaust undoubtedly flows through Gene's veins. And it is the strength of people like Flora that we must never forget; for it is that strength which ultimately triumphed over the hate and evil of that dark time."

-Chris A. White
Founder: KissAsylum.com

"Gene must have learned from his mother that the power of the mind and staying positive and working hard will lead to a successful life."

-Lynn Goldsmith
KISS Photographer

flash pots and talcum powder

By 1974, the members of KISS had been together as a band for less than a year. It was early yet, and they were still experimenting with their outfits, stage moves, set lists, and theatrical alter-egos. The clubs they played were dark and dingy and the employees often outnumbered the audience members, but things were looking up; Paul had finally settled on his star design and the band discovered that talcum powder was the secret ingredient to keeping long hair from sticking to face make-up.

The act was still very much a jewel in the rough, but Gene felt confident enough in their recent progress to warrant an invitation to his beloved mother to see a show. Flora arrived at the weeknight gig to witness the band squeezed onto a tiny stage that arched under the weight of amplified equipment and glowed beneath a stylish logo. Glancing warily at the flashing Nazi lightning bolts, Flora deliberately averted her eyes from the offending SS design and watched as the group gave it their all. Paul pouted his lips and played the role of sex symbol while Ace fell to his knees like a teetering space alien. Gene's thrusting tongue gave him the appearance of a demonic lizard as Peter battered his drum kit with animal intensity. The 20 minute set concluded with four loud flashpots and the band disappearing to a backstage changing area to remove their warpaint. Emerging with faces freshly scrubbed and in casual street clothes, the boys cordially greeted Mrs. Klein and excused themselves to sit at the bar. Gene put his arm around Flora and gently walked her towards the door.

"Well mom….what did you think?"

"Oh Chaim, your orchestra was wonderful."

"Did you find each band member to be unique and exciting?"

"Oh yes. I loved it. Which one were **you**?"

"As an 8th grade Middle School student in Terre Haute, the Diary of Anne Frank was required reading. Though the most disturbing images, for me, came from a film the teachers showed us. To this day, it was worse than anything Hollywood could ever create, because it was real. The film was shot after the war showing what the soldiers found when they came to the concentration camps. I saw broken, disfigured, skeleton-like cadavers being dumped into a ditch by a tractor which became a mass grave - disregarding the fact that these remains were once human beings. I saw some of the survivors who seemed almost skeleton-like themselves behind a barbed wire fence. Their expressions looked like, though they had survived, they had "died" inside. The cruelty and the suffering were evident throughout the film. Decades later, those sickening images from the film still haunt me today. In my day to day life, I am a teacher. When it comes to the Holocaust, the most horrible atrocity of the past 100 years, we all become teachers. It is our duty, our responsibility, as teachers to make sure this crime against humanity is never repeated and never forgotten. God tells us to forgive but we must never forget to teach future generations about this part of history. I am honored to be included in this inspirational endeavor that celebrates the life of one of the legendary figures of Rock and Roll and American pop culture and his mother, both, as true survivors in the shadows of the Holocaust."

-Bill Starkey
Founder: The KISS Army

a twinship

Many years before circumstances in Terre Haute, Indiana, helped lead to the establishment of the state of Israel - - the city was simply an undeveloped patch of territory on a plateau aside the Wabash River. Settlers struggled to tame the land. Speculators struggled to fill unsold lots and collect unpaid loans. Farmers and Millers struggled to transport their products southward. In 1823, 'The Steamboat Florence' ushered in a new era of river transportation -- putting Terre Haute on the map forever; fostering travel, increasing business, and jumpstarting the city's overall range of influence. As the labor market exploded, a massive growth in population occurred; the largest group being German immigrants who went about laboring on the canal and surrounding rail networks. It was a 'Do It Yourself' affair in the pioneer tradition. And the pioneer tradition doesn't recognize "No" as a fixed reality.

You see, No is only No until the next time you ask. Flora said this often. Her son took it to heart. As a boy, Chaim Witz doggedly peddled his goods to his fussy countrymen in Haifa, Israel. As a teenager, Gene Klein sold his wares in the bustling streets of Queens, New York. He wrote his songs and consigned them to tape; submitting them proudly to A & R Reps. He hatched creepy tales and fantasy drawings and mailed them to the best Monster Mags. A myriad of rejection letters arrived in response. Gene savored and studied the advice they contained and set about better refining his craft. The more vehement the rejection, the greater Gene's determination to re-submit an improved product. As a young adult, Gene Simmons harvested a vast collection of music biz contacts and kept them apprised of his band's every move.

A steady barrage.

Stamped and addressed with ferocious regularity.

Bordering on harassment.

Gene seized every opportunity; and when opportunities were slim, he created his own.

Gene made money and he saved money.

Lifeguard.

Paper Boy.

Publisher's Assistant.

Grade School Teacher.

He purchased equipment then rented it out to competing bands.

His discipline and savings allowed for a pivotal rehearsal loft. Transportation to and from gigs.

And an ability to self-book hotel ballrooms to publicly showcase KISS in its infancy.

It was a 'Do It Yourself' affair and it paid off quickly. Management. Record label. Stardom.

And fans.

Rabid

Fiercely

dedicated

Maniacally loyal
F   A   N   A   T   I   C   S
"You guys better start playing some KISS records or we're gonna surround the building."
Radio station WVTS was inundated.
Night and day.
A steady barrage.
Phone lines rang with ferocious regularity.
Bordering on harassment.
Seizing every opportunity.
We may just be a bunch of kids - - but there's enough of us to start an army.

The town took notice. The DJ's wouldn't budge. But No is only No until the next time you ask. And senior high school student Bill Starkey wasn't waiting for permission. He was the ringleader of the 'KISS Army'. The self-appointed General of a self-created fan club. A 'Do It Yourself' affair in the pioneer tradition.

Something was happening in Terre Haute, Indiana. The powerless had become the powerful. The duality resonated with one Gene Simmons: Comic Book Enthusiast.

In the illustrated stories that Gene devoured, an over-riding theme was ever present: the notion of twinship; the idea that every hero has a dual identity -- a powerless self living a normal everyday life and a power*ful* self with secret super powers.

A twinship.

Like the one that allowed mild mannered reporter

Clark Kent to change into Superman.

Like the one that allowed fish-out-of-water immigrant Chaim Klein to metamorphose into The Bat Lizard.

Like the one that allowed a laid back, humble high school kid named Bill Starkey to transmogrify into The Founder and General of The KISS Army; to establish a National Fan Club Headquarters and bring the band to his beloved town of Terre Haute. Where they would be welcomed by marching bands and military escorts and a key to the city. Where they would handily sell out Hulman Center -- a feat previously accomplished only by the great Elvis Presley. Another boy who lost himself in fantasy to control his terrors. Another Jew - courtesy of his mother's genealogical bloodline. Another rags-to-riches story of a powerless boy who looked to comic books to unlock the powerful twinship that resides within a single person. A surviving twin obligated to make it up to the non-surviving twin. A life lived with a keen understanding of one's own triumphant survival.

A realization that the powerful must protect the powerless.

A life lived big to achieve for the dead. The guilt and burden of a child called 'Life'. The guilt and burden of the twinless twin.

A fascination to humankind since the first set were born to Isaac and Rebekah in Genesis 25:25-26, Terre Haute housed a museum devoted exclusively to twins. To the twins who served as the dehumanized test subjects of Dr. Josef Mengele. The CANDLES Museum. Short for "Children of Auschwitz Nazi Deadly Lab Experiments Survivors". Ordained to the young victims of vile Nazi experimentation. A plea, a reminder, and a challenge to the world to forget not the past or be at risk to ever repeat it. Gene somberly viewed the brick-lined structure through a car window as he left the Wabash Valley. The party was over. For his pioneering spirit, Bill Starkey was presented a plaque before a crowd of ten thousand. And now Gene's limo was ready to roll out of town. In the rear window, the CANDLES Museum shrunk in size but followed him like an unshakable moon on a long evening's journey; like a determined child chases the family car, running and waving.

A muted cry.

A lingering scent.

The stench of Mengele's deeds; so deeply foul in their profound, profound evil. A Man of Medicine injecting needles into the eyeballs of children. Amputating their limbs and stuffing wood shavings into their open wounds. Sewing separate bodies together back to back; wrist to wrist. Live autopsies. Shock treatments. Typhus injections. He burned children alive in giant pits; strolling the perimeter with a stick to push back those who struggled to climb out.

A Man of Medicine.

Determined to unlock the secrets of replica features contained within twins.

Determined to genetically engineer the population of Europe to Aryan perfection.

Determined but successful only in carrying out wholly unscientific experiments on innocent children and leaving unspeakable pain, torture, and carnage in his wake.

When the war ended, the once omnipotent Dr. Mengele scurried into hiding like a frightened cockroach. The powerful had become the powerless.

Poverty replaced wealth.

Scorn replaced fame.

Anonymity replaced station.

Fear replaced brazen entitlement.

Hard labor replaced ruling privilege.

In Auschwitz, Mengele decided who would live and who would die with the careless motion of a single finger. Now, he was a hunted man; friendless, terrified, living in squalor. For the next 35 years of his wretched life.

Existing in the shadows, Mengele watched as the world transformed around him. Germany expressed its shame and begged the world for forgiveness. Israel became a mighty Jewish homeland. Former Nazis were imprisoned and executed for their crimes. And Mengele – who dreamed of being loved, respected, and celebrated throughout the remainder of recorded history as "The Father of Genetic Engineering" – now found himself the object of the medical community's greatest contempt: ridiculed, reviled, mocked and loathed as a quack, a fool, an anathema, and a monster. The name Mengele was on par with that of Satan himself.

In the final decades of his life, Dr. Mengele lived in unseizing physical pain. A spinal injury, broken hip, and enlarged prostate gave him no rest as he lay on a hard stone floor under a battered roof that leaked when it rained. As he suffered a stroke whilst swimming that final day, Mengele was slowly and agonizingly strangled by the ocean's waves. As the water took its own sweet time suffocating the doctor that afternoon, one wonders if Mengele gave any thought to the slow agonizing pain he himself had inflicted on others -- to the despicably cruel manner in which he had brought death upon his victims. One wonders about the nature of Humankind -- with all its capacity to think and build and solve and create; with all its capacity for love and brilliance and art and beauty……..and all its capacity for hate and cruelty and stupidity and destruction. Nine million people murdered. Six million Jews. Countless numbers of traumatized, physically and psychologically battered survivors. One wonders about the Holocaust. And the nature of Humankind.

Could it ever happen again?

No.

Of course, No is only No until the next time you ask.

Concentration Camp North of Berlin
(photos courtesy of the Berg family)

Concentration Camp North of Berlin
(photo courtesy of the Berg family)

Haifa, Israel - Gene's birthplace and early home
(photo courtesy of the Berg family)

**Apartment building Gene lived in with his mother Flora
in the 1960's, Jackson Heights, New York**
(photos courtesy of Daniel Hill - www.kissinuk.com)

Gene's Junior High School in Jackson Heights, New York
(photo courtesy of Daniel Hill - www.kissinuk.com)

One of many Fanzines that Gene created and contributed to in the 1960's
(from the author's personal collection)

Fanzines Gene created and contributed to in the 1960's
(from the author's personal collection)

Fanzines that Gene created and contributed to in the 1960's
(from the author's personal collection)

"Klein's Komic Komments":
One of Gene's Fanzine editorial corners from the 1960's
(from the author's personal collection)

One of many Fanzines that Gene created and contributed to in the 1960's
(from the author's personal collection)

Gene's High School in Flushing, New York
(photo courtesy of Daniel Hill - www.kissinuk.com)

"Max's Kansas City" poster advertisement
(photo courtesy of the author)

Where Gene taught 6th grade - PS 75 in Spanish Harlem, New York
(photo courtesy of Daniel Hill - www.kissinuk.com)

Where Gene taught 6th grade - PS 75 in Spanish Harlem, New York
(photo courtesy of Daniel Hill - www.kissinuk.com)

Bill Starkey - Founder of the KISS Army
(photo courtesy of Bill Starkey)

A cute - - and rather accurate - - cartoon by artist Benjamin Boling

(courtesy of B.E. Boling - www.bennygraphix.com)

Manhattan Apartment where Gene and Cher lived together
(photo courtesy of Daniel Hill - www.kissinuk.com)

Lobby of the Manhattan Apartment where Gene and Cher lived together
(photo courtesy of Daniel Hill - www.kissinuk.com)

'Children of Auschwitz Nazi Deadly Lab Experiments Survivors'
C.A.N.D.L.E.S. Museum in Terre Haute, Indiana
(photo courtesy of Eva Kor - Survivor and Museum Founder)

Yad Vashem Holocaust Museum in Israel
(photo courtesy of the Berg family)

Gene Simmons

Gene and Flora

(Photo Courtesy of Ross Halfin
Copyright: All Rights Reserved
http://rosshalfin.com/home/intro.php)

"Through the midst of tragedy came a little woman named Florence. She would give birth to a baby boy. It was a life that started out very simple. But he grew to be a man who showed the masses that knowledge is power and no star is unreachable; no dream untouchable. And he carved out his own place in the pages of history to become the legend he is today."

-Barry Carr
Artist & Designer: KISS Costume
Replication

"Gene was persecuted and preyed upon by the school bullies for being different; well, he ended up having the last laugh by attaining success beyond anyone's wildest dreams."

-Evan E. Rotman
Chef, Culinary Activist, Psychedelic
Warrior

if i look lost

"I've got a new rock group for you, Totie", talk show host Mike Douglas announced for the benefit of his previous guest as much as for the audience watching at home. "Before we see them perform, I want you to meet one of the members of this act close up", Douglas stated with a concerned expression. "Here, from KISS, is Gene Simmons." Greeted by audience laughter and audible groans of disgust, Gene walked onto the set in full demon warpaint and took his seat awkwardly between the tv host and comedienne Totie Fields. Dressed in black leather, batwings, and devil horns protruding from behind his shoulders - Gene felt his boots filling up with sweat as he nervously tried to get through the experience.

"Incidentally, he's up for adoption" cracked Totie, rolling her eyes in disgust.

The audience roared with laughter as Gene nervously sunk lower into his chair.

Totie was on a roll.

"Is your mother watching today?"

Simmons, taken aback, replied softly: "I hope so." Fields then spoke to Douglas as if Gene were no longer in the room, "Wouldn't it be funny if under this, he was just a nice Jewish boy?" The audience members chuckled and exchanged glances. "You should only know", Gene mumbled. "I *do* know", she shot back. "You can't hide the hook."

They all laughed.

And it was true. He *couldn't* hide the hook. And he couldn't hide the fact that he couldn't speak a word of English either.

They bullied him and they laughed and pointed their fingers. They snatched the yarmulke from his head. At school, they pinned a sign on his back:

IF I LOOK LOST, POINT ME IN THE RIGHT DIRECTION

They held him back a grade. They thought him a fool. Visuals became his only friends: comic book art, colorful monster movie creatures, Disney cartoons; whatever images he could connect with sans language. He excelled at the non-verbal game of marbles, played silent cowboys in school plays, displayed his tongue to girls for reaction, drew pictures to express his ideas and his dreams, and ultimately used his painted face to communicate with people around the world of every culture and language imaginable.

"So, what are you supposed to be?" asked a perplexed Mike Douglas. His audience of middle-aged housewives were now howling; confident in the fact that this man would amount to nothing.

He would amount to becoming the biggest rock star of the decade.

He would succeed in conveying fantasy, freedom, and dream fulfillment the world over through pure visual communication. He would never forget the name Totie Fields; listing her amongst others on his platinum solo record. Thanking her for being just one more bully to prove wrong, perhaps.

"Five minutes to showtime, Gene!" hollered the Stage Manager.

"Is your mother watching tonight?"

The stadium was filled to capacity and Gene peered out at the faces from the side of the stage. "I hope so", he replied softly.

"It's no coincidence that Comic Books were born in the midst of the Second World War. Characters like Superman, Batman and Captain America gave Jews an outlet to write about identity, rage, and, most importantly, hope. The history of Jews and Comic Books are more intertwined than my Grandmother's Shabbat Challah."

-Daniel Levitch
Creative Director: "Ancient Squid Media"

"Comics have been around in one form or another for thousands of years. They're older than the Bible. Moses grew up in Egypt, after all, surrounded by palaces and temples covered with words and pictures meant to be read together. And that's how words and pictures work best."

-Adam Black
The KISS 4K Comic Book Series

"I remember being seven or eight years old when I discovered Gene Simmons in a magazine. While I was initially very scared of him, he became my idol. To me, he was bigger than Superman, Batman, and the Incredible Hulk all rolled into one."

-Craig Boyce
Co-Founder: God of Thunder Facebook Page

tuesdays with stan lee

"There is a point of discussion I would like to address."

"Okay. I'm in a bit of a hurry, but okay."

"I have always been curious, Mr. Lee...."

"Please, call me Stan."

"Okay, Stan. Yeah. Listen, Stan. In issue 6 of Captain America - - what was the creative spark behind the double-page illustration replacing the standard nine panels per page?"

"Oh fer cryin' out - - I don't remember, Gene! That was an eternity ago. We're talkin' about **the 1940's......**"

The decade that introduced Batman, Robin, Superboy, Wonder Woman, The Flash, The Green Lantern, Plastic Man, Aquaman, The Human Torch, Captain America.

And a boy named Chaim.

Born in 1949, he was a grade school kid through the next ten years and a young adult in the ten after that.

Three decades.

The forties. The fifties. And the sixties. The most crucial 30 years in the popularity and cultural influence of comic books.

Where radio used only verbal descriptions and theater action was limited by a stage and movies were often in black and white and televisions were grainy and crackling with static - - comic books delivered grand adventure and riveting escapism in vibrant living color. Fellow entertainment providers were limited by budgets and primitive special effects. Comic book creators were limited only by their story ideas and drawing abilities. From the 1940's through the late 1960's, the competitors of the comic book never stood a fighting chance.

As a devotee of art forms free from real-life restrictions and limitations, Chaim Witz was born at the right time. As a Jew from another country, he was a member of a tribe of comic book creators and superhero characters. Many of them posing as gentiles. Many of them harboring dual identities. Real-life Clark Kents writing and illustrating a universe of Supermen. Strangers in a strange land. Visitors from another world. Gene found these figures to be a source of great comfort. He felt a special kinship with them. A true sense of vicarious empowerment. They mirrored his status and struggles as an immigrant. The creators and their creations both.

Superman was a particular favorite.

"Okay Stan…..Superman 12. Page 6. Panel 3. Existential symbolism or printing error? Talk to me."

"Oh fer crying out loud!"

Created by two Jews in the 1930's, the Man of Steel served as a wish-fulfillment fantasy to Jewish kids the world over. He was the quintessential American hero. And the quintessential metaphor for the Jewish experience. His real name was Kal-El, meaning 'Vessel of God' in Hebrew. He came to America as a refugee to escape a mass holocaust of his people. Just as many German Jews sent their children on kindertransports to seek sanctuary with other families, Kal-El's parents placed him in a vessel and propelled him to safety like baby Moses in a basket of reeds on the Nile. Both Kal-El and Moses were discovered by new parents and raised in cultures foreign to their own. When the two boys became men, their spiritual guides beseeched them to assist humanity and save their people. Both Superman and Moses kept their true identities a secret - - with Superman living a double life as Clark Kent. Attempting to attain the Immigrant Ideal of cultural assimilation, Clark is nonetheless a bespectacled nebbish in the tradition of Jewish stereotypes complete with the stammering speech pattern of Moses.

Just as the Golem was created to defend the Jews from their anti-Semitic enemies, Superman too was created to do battle with Hitler within the pages of his illustrated adventures. And he wasn't the only one. Soon, a virtual army of superheroes were lining up to beat the hell out of the Nazis. An army of heroes with dual identities and Jewish characteristics. Written and illustrated by Jews.

Before becoming Batman, Bruce Wayne watched helplessly as his parents were gunned down in the streets; a scene horrifyingly reminiscent of post-Holocaust Jews who witnessed the generation before them slain throughout the city streets of Europe. Batman went on to battle Nazis in a multitude of comic adventures throughout the 1940's. Captain Marvel Jr. took on a character called Captain Nazi while Captain America punched out Hitler himself.

And the Nazi poundings continued through the efforts of Doc Strange, V-Man, Uncle Sam, Captain Marvel, Minute Man, Captain Flag, The Hangman, Sub-Mariner, The Black Terror, The Shield, and The Spy Smasher. In the tradition of the Tribes of Israel, The Justice League of America emphasized the collective strengths of a group in its fight against evil forces. The Green Lantern's Guardian's of the Universe were modeled after Israeli Prime Minister David Ben-Gurion. The Hulk and The Thing were Golemesque figures; with the latter being known to chant the Hebrew Kaddish prayer. The Atom celebrated Chanukah. Spiderman Peter Parker suffered guilt on a level rivaling any Jew on the planet. And Magneto was a Holocaust survivor.

In 1939, Superman fought to keep poison gas from being obtained and used by a Hitleresque character in issue #2. This led real-life Nazi Minister of

Propaganda Josef Goebbels to lash out at the comic book character, denouncing him as a Jew. Goebbels was clearly irked; the Jews succeeded where Hitler had failed: they created an Ubermensch. A super man. They beat the Nazis to it. And didn't kill a single child in the process.

"Stan, when you created the first Spiderman comic book…"

"Gene, let's stay focused on creating the first *KISS* comic book."

Gene Simmons. Comic Book Superhero.
This was the defining moment.
A culmination.
Born out of fatherlessness and social isolation. Born out of three decades worth of life events that hurt too much to repeat and attention-getting experiences that proved too intoxicating not to refine and master for future use.
Looking back, Reptillicus was a light in the darkness. When it hit American movie theatres, Gene was entranced as the prehistoric fantasy creature stalked the big screen - - flicking it's enormous tongue in and out of a mouth teeming with green acid. Thrilled by the spectacle he witnessed, Gene sat in school the next day - - flicking and extending his tongue as he played and replayed the movie in his mind. Momentarily losing himself in an impermeable zone

of make-believe, he rolled his eyes inside of his head and swirled his tongue from side to side. Disgusted yet titillated by the spectacle she witnessed, the girl behind him let out a scream and teacher sent Gene to Detention Hall. In one fell swoop, Gene's electrifying fantasy performance earned him both female attention and respect from the cool kids for pissing off authority. This was validation. Gene had hit on something.

In Junior High School, another glow arrived to illuminate the dusk. Gene was a chubby little boy when 'The Twist' became a hit single. By the time it spawned a national dance craze -- Gene was, at best, ignored; at worst, viciously ridiculed. But something changed. The music triggered an untapped talent that revealed itself as an important social tool. The boy could dance. He could really move. Gene entered a Twist Contest and won. Suddenly, the girls began to look twice and the boys greeted him in the hallways.

The road seemed clear:
Fantasy and Music.
They had both provided attention, respect, and praise.
They had both provided feelings of power and of social connection.
They had both provided an avenue to feel unique and special from the others.
Like a first tiny taste of fame.
Yes, Gene had definitely hit on something.

And he liked it.

He liked it so very, very much.

Fantasy and Music.

It seemed to him now that a perfectly balanced marriage of the two could provide a bottomless well of ego gratification. This could be a rocket to the moon. His ticket out. The phone booth that grants Clark Kent entry to exit as Superman. This was a golden pass to the future. Where Gene would join the ranks of Spiderman and Batman as an animated hero in the pages of his own comic book.

The time was now.

1977. A new decade of fantasy built on the three that preceded it. 30 years of glorious escape and adventure. Of heroes and villains and cops and robbers and alter egos and tights and capes and mild and mannered and murder and mayhem and social satire and tales of terror.

"Stan, when I was a kid I wrote a letter to you about my goals and dreams and you sent me back a postcard saying 'Never give up'".

"Is that right, Gene? Well I'll be damned".

Tuesdays with Stan Lee. The Head of Marvel Comics. The Creator of Spiderman. A fellow Jew with a dual identity who had changed his name in order to assimilate. The man whose Black Bolt character influenced Gene's batwing costume design. Stan Lee. Bursting with imagination. Seeing the possibilities. A kindred spirit. The two men discussed story ideas and marketing strategies for the KISS comic book. They shared notions of character development and pacing. They spoke of the Jews and their unique role in the origins of the modern comic book. They talked well into the night.

Released the following year, the KISS comic book became the biggest-selling title in the entire history of Marvel Comics.

Now Gene himself would serve as a source of comfort and vicarious empowerment to the next wave of youth; to the next crop of strangers in strange lands, visitors from other worlds, and invisible introverts living secret lives and dual identities. Gene had dreamed of living inside the "Mr. Make Believe" that resided in the song he had written as a young man; by doing so, he had emerged as the Mr. Make Believe that the next generation wanted to live inside. This was a great responsibility. And, to hear Spiderman tell it, something that must always accompany great power.

"I believe that without Gene's work ethic, there would be no KISS. He eats, lives, breathes KISS 24/7 and has since the inception of the band."
-Mike Shupe
Co-Founder: The KISS Detention Hall

"Gene Simmons is a marketing genius. He is the John Wayne of Rock 'N Roll. He could have been a major political leader. Gene is focused in such a way that he leaves the competition in the dust."
-Kim Fowley
Record Producer, Impresario,
Musician, Film Maker, and Radio Actor
KISS Songwriting Collaborator

"Gene is the biggest workaholic I've ever seen. It's probably why KISS became the most popular band on the planet'.
-Steven Mitchell
Host - Salt Lake City KISS Night

mazel tov

"Hello?"

"Hi mom, it's Gene…"

"Oh Chaim! How is my darling son?"

"Good, we just got back from Japan. We played four nights at Budokan and broke attendance records set by the Beatles. Unbelievable. We brought the full crew with us and eleven journalists. The set cost over $80,000. It was a riot…we got there and 5,000 fans surrounded us and Japanese officials made us take off our make-up so we could show the proper identification. The fans just went *crazy* for us. Just insane."

"Mazel tov."

"So we just signed with Boutwell. They're projecting we'll bring in about two million dollars within a year. T-shirts. Necklaces. Posters. Tour books. Belt buckles. The works. Millions of dollars. Our faces on everything. Your son's face on t-shirts from here to Japan and back again ten times over."

"My darling son."

"The first comic book was huge and so they're

working on another for next year. 1978 is gonna be **the** year for KISS, mom. We'll be adapting the KISS comic book storyline for our first movie. They're giving us a two million dollar budget. 'Star Wars' meets 'Hard Day's Night'. Your son is gonna be a movie star, ma. And get this - - - by the end of Fall, we're all doing solo records. Four solo albums released at the same time. This is unprecedented. Absolutely unprecedented in the music business."

"Mazel tov, Chaim."

"And we were just voted the top rock band in the world. It's a Gallup thing. The Gallup Poll. We were voted the best. Above the Stones, the Beatles, Boston, Zeppelin….really big names, mom. They tell me there's gonna be new Halloween costumes and a KISS Christmas television special. Last night on the plane I was talking to management about something called "KISS World". Sort of like a traveling amusement park, mom. You see, this would be something that kids could enjoy in the time before the show….you know….in the hours leading up to the concert. There would be rides and games and everything would be KISS. A Gene Simmons rollercoaster and a Peter Criss petting zoo or what-have-you. Ace Frehley space rides or whatever. So we're in discussions now. But yeah, Boutwell's gonna be doing KISS garbage pails and notebooks. They say it's gonna bring in about two million dollars a year.

But, yeah. So I just got back from Japan last night."

"That's wonderful, Chaim. I am so proud. So what else are you working on?"

"I was just starting out as a young photographer and was sent on the road with KISS. The band's manager mostly just wanted me along so I could babysit Ace Frehley and make sure he didn't drink too much before KISS had to play onstage."
-Richard E. Aaron
KISS Photographer

"When you lose your power as a child, you typically seek to find control later in your adult life."
-Jeff Alan Brekich
Member: The Flora Army

"The Holocaust was a way to segregate and intimidate people in a very authoritative manor, in which one had no choice. Rock and Roll is a free choice and becomes a common bond, like family, to all those who embrace it, even when the people are of different cultures. It hits home in one's heart."
-Rock And Roll Over – KISS Tribute Band

never forget to remember

There was a commotion.

Surrounding guests emerged from their rooms. A steel-toed boot kicked the door. "Who is it? What do you want?" questioned a voice from inside the room.

"Zeig Heil!", the man yelled, dressed in Nazi regalia from head to toe – kicking the door again.

A deadbolt thunked and the door handle turned and a figure in the darkened room wore an expression of deep, bitter disappointment.

"Goddamnit, Ace! What the *hell* are you doing?"

Ace exploded into delirious laughter – very drunk and very much in the mood to be silly.

A crowd of bewildered hotel guests filled the hallway as Gene spoke into the telephone. "Eddie, come up to my room and get this idiot out of here." The band's bodyguard arrived to escort Frehley from the premises. "I'll put him to bed, Gene. He'll never remember this in the morning."

Ace would never remember.

Gene would never forget.

Ace would relinquish control of his senses. Gene would never surrender control.

Never again to be muted and powerless. Never again to be poor.

And walking up Madison Avenue to 60th, Flora arrived every week to receive. To receive and methodically tally. Stacks and stacks of mounds of greenbacks. Courtesy of her only son. And the office staff undoubtedly saw her. Executives and clerical workers alike. Did they laugh to themselves? And crack wise in silent sarcasm: "Now *there's* a rare sight -- a Jew counting money." Did they realize that long ago the Jews were forced to be money-lenders? Forced by Christians forbidden by The Church to charge interest? Forced to be money-lenders and then despised for it and blamed for the world's problems? Did they realize that? Well, that's okay. Let them laugh. And let them see. They could think what they wanted but no one would ever fuck with his mother again. He was the boss now. And his mother would only ever be treated with the reverence and respect that she had *always* deserved in the first place. In the Camps, she had spent her days fishing lunch from the garbage. In the Bronx, she had hand-picked lint off the clothing of the rich. Now she was the boss' mother and she deserved only to receive. Reverance, respect, and...... her sons' money. And plenty of it. And count it up, ma. Nice and slow. Take the afternoon if you need it. Make sure every penny is present and accounted for. It's for you, mom. It's all for you. Always has been. Let them see you count it. Let them know. Let them take it all in. Wads of cash. From the floor up to the popcorn ceiling. A fixer. A glue. A glorious instrument yielding food and shelter and protection for mother. The son is now the father. The husband who never was. He who left his wife and child penniless and in the streets to starve to death for all he cared. He is fully erased and replaced. By the boy.

The boy.

Mother had suffered and struggled and scrimped and survived. For her boy. Everything for the boy. And he had so much to do now. So much to achieve. So much to share. So much to repay. So he showered her with riches. His mother. His Queen.

And he had no use for drugs. And he had not time for drink. They dulled your senses and drained your wallet and muted your talents and broke your Jewish mother's heart.

And eroded control.

He had first discovered it when he came to America as a boy. When his black and white world turned to color and he lost himself in the beautiful fantasy of movies and comics and make-believe and the light turned on his brain and said: "There can be even more."

There could be more.

He could now see possibilities and dream even bigger dreams. There could be more and he felt something special. A driving force. A sense of purpose. A sense of control.

There could be more but only if he mastered control.

After all, a Jew at the mercy of society was a dangerous and precarious proposition; a thing proven disastrous throughout history and time. And most of them realized it. Most of them recognized that the sturdy SS Man's claims were farcical: "Nothing will happen to you! Simply take a deep breath inside the chambers. This will expand your lungs and retard illness and infection." Some felt a glimmer of hope, but the majority realized. They understood. They knew. Zyklon B. A pesticide. It poured through the openings in the ceilings. And they screamed in agony and dug their fingers into the walls. Eight hundred at a time pressed together on 25 square meters. Women and children. Dead. And still standing. Like stone statues. Like basalt pillars. Standing on each other's feet. There had been no room to fall down. And so they stood in death. Families. Their hands still clasped. Their frozen embraces finally pried from one another with hooks to make room for the next load of women holding their babies.

No. Ceding control was not an option. Not for him.

Not for his people. Never again.

Power. Money. Influence. Control.

These things would keep him safe.

He prayed to God they would keep him safe.

How to get there? Something pointed the way. He knew he could sing. And he knew his guitar. He knew he could draw and he knew he could write. He knew his imagination was strong. And 'no' was never an option.

And he knew how to hide. How to perform. How to live inside an armor shell of his making and to grow strong from it. To defuse his Golem when it threatened to overtake him. To become all-powerful. To be in control of his audience. To be in control of his life. And the future.

And when that future included visits from men who had lost control of their faculties -- a simple phone call would be placed to promptly remove such men from his sight.

"I'll put him to bed, Gene. He'll never remember this in the morning."

But Gene would always remember.

To forget was not an option.

For him *or* his people.

"I was about three years old when my mom started dating Gene. We were all crazy about him. My sister Chastity spent most of her youth in KISS make-up."

-Elijah Blue Allman
Son of Singer/Actress Cher

"Seven inch leather heels, outrageous make-up and costumes, hair bigger than your sister....that's KISS! The fire, the bombs, the catchy rock and roll tunes.... that's KISS! They are as Seventies as David Bowie or Alice Cooper, but times FOUR! They are as iconic as Star Wars. They are what made 70's Pop Culture so popular all over the world....they are KISS!"

-Danny Casaboontha
Casaboontha Rock Music Designs

"Gene Simmons is a very caring, loving and devoted father."

-Janelle Bowen
Member: "The Flora Army"

like the blur of a skater goes round and around

At the Glickman/Marks Management office on 75 East 55th Street in New York, phone calls and stacks of mail poured in ceaselessly. The office staff diligently tended to all messages, media correspondence, fan club orders, and special requests from friends and relatives of the band. At the end of every long day, the majority of telephone calls were returned and every stack of mail was significantly reduced in height. Except one. One stack of mail always grew taller and never smaller. It was a specific stack of mail. Sent to Gene from his father. A man he had not seen or heard from in 17 years. A man whose sudden interest in fatherly duties seemed to coincide perfectly with his son's newfound fame and fortune. No, this particular stack of letters would remain unopened. Unanswered. Untouched.

In passing years, for reasons never supplied – Gene dispatched an assistant to the Holy Land to purchase a home for his father. Whether this was a declaration of love, a display of who was the better man, or something else entirely was never clarified. In any event, despite this purchase – in all those years, from the son to the father – never a word was spoken; never a letter was written; never a glance was bestowed. When the old man died, a beautiful song was penned by the surviving son of the deceased. A tender eulogy. "Now That You're Gone". Decades later, Gene visited his father's gravesite in Israel and openly wept at the man's passing - - the Hebrew writing on the headstone confirming the finality of the old man's death.

The coffin was sealed.

The dirt was in place.

There would be no reconciliation.

Where his mother was his entire world - his protector, his teacher, his inspiration, his hero - Gene Simmons would never know his father personally.

"I KNOW GENE SIMMONS PERSONALLY!!"

Upon reading these words on the young girl's sweatshirt, Gene hugged her tightly and laughed with joy. Although the youngster's mother had sold over 80 million records worldwide and was nominated for 15 Emmy Awards as one half of "Sonny and Cher", the girl really wasn't particularly impressed. Cher was just mom.

But Gene Simmons was an
otherworldly
larger than life
wild-eyed
half man
half lizard
superhero
rock god
returning with the tablets from the Mountain.

He also loved a good food fight and could well end up being the girl's new father if all continued to go well with her mother.

Attending one of Cher's annual skating parties did not much appeal to Gene, but he came to the event with a smile feeling that, at age 27, he was in love for the first time in his life. Watching the skaters from a chair in the corner of the room, Gene nodded politely as the guests rolled past him. Round and round. Over and over. A blur of medallions and polyester. He felt out of place. The skaters whooped and hollered as the disco hits of the day pulsed with measured steadiness from two enormous speakers. 120 beats a minute. Over and over. A blur of rhythmic sameness. Gene felt out of place. To his slight relief, he saw two bouncing mops of teenage hair heading in his direction. Upon viewing the KISS shirts the boys were wearing, he felt his shoulders relaxing for the first time that evening. "Wow, Gene Simmons, man!"

"Yeah, can we get yer autograph, Gene?" Grinning widely, Gene took the taller boy's pen and began to sign as the younger one asked, "Is it true that you had a cow's tongue sewn over your real one?"

Laughing, Gene's response to the question was cut short at the sight of a man now standing a few feet behind the boys - checking his watch and appearing somewhat antsy.

Gene swallowed hard as he instantly recognized the familiar curves and features of the man's face. Those warm eyes. Those thick lips. That nose.

Gene, along with 74 million other people, had

watched this man playing drums one Sunday night on the Ed Sullivan Show back in 1964. Smiling and clobbering his drum kit, he sported the same suit and hairstyle worn by the three guitar players performing in front of him. Ed Sullivan had introduced them as 'The Beatles' and their music and their energy was intoxicating; causing the girls in the audience to cry and scream and faint in the aisles. A teenaged Gene moved closer to the television set to soak this all in. Narrowing his eyes and licking his lips, the gears in his brain clicked into place like a student who suddenly understands Calculus. This was more than just music. This group looked like no one else on the planet. Sure, the drummer with the droopy eyes and the silly grin was different from the cute pudgy-faced bass player with the violin-shaped guitar -- but those were minor details: the important thing was these guys were all from the same 'Beatle Mother'. And that was the rub. Gene knew this group had come up with a great idea; maybe he could do them one better.

And so here he sat. 1977. A multimillionaire dating a world-famous actress. The leader of KISS. Named by Gallup Poll as the single most popular rock band in existence. Ranked above The Beatles. Breaking concert attendance records set by The Beatles. More merchandised than The Beatles. More recognizable than The Beatles. Heck, the members of KISS had their faces patented through the Trademark Office of the United States of America. In the eyes of many fans and observers of popular culture, Gene **had** done The Beatles one better.

And as he fielded questions from the teenage boys in the skating rink ~*Does KISS really stand for 'Knights In Satan's Service?'*~ Gene craned his neck and struggled to get a better look at the famous drummer -- one of the four men on Ed Sullivan's stage that night responsible for igniting so many of the dreams he had now fulfilled. "Uh, excuse me guys - I've enjoyed chatting with you but I'd like to try and introduce myself to Ringo back there before he leaves."

The two boys glanced over their shoulders and turned back to Gene with confused expressions.

"*Him*?" the older boy asked.

"Yeah, he's one of my heroes. Haven't you guys ever heard of Ringo Starr?"

"Well, yeah, we've heard of him -- he's our **dad**. But, *big deal*? You're **Gene Simmons**! The God of Thunder! You're a **LEGEND**; he's just dad."

Gene was speechless.

And the disco hits of the day continued. Two years on, the beat continued. The loves of his life and the years rolled past him. Cher was replaced by a lovely Supreme like the blur of a skater goes round and around. And as the decade rapidly came to a close, the disco ball ruled -- shining brightest on three brothers called Gibb. Seven Grammy Awards. 120 million albums sold. The biggest soundtrack recording in the history of the music industry. The elder

Gibb had written five of the Top Ten singles the year that "Saturday Night Fever" was nominated for an Academy Award and who did his son want to meet? "Gene Simmons!" the boy yelled, "You're the greatest! The God of Thunder!!"

And the conversation proceeded the way it always did:

He's just my dad/You're a star

As a boy, Gene would have been content to have had a father who simply loved him enough to have remained in his life. Celebrity or no.

It still hurt.

And in the darkness of the movie theatre, Gene watched the screen with tears streaming down his face as the beautiful woman arrived at Auschwitz with her family. The images assaulted his senses. The squalor of the Jewish Ghettos. The serial numbers tattooed on body parts. The thick smoke that poured out of Crematorium Two. The gut-wrenching choices to be made. In many ways, he felt he was watching his mother's story that day. Alone in the darkness. He decided then that if God ever blessed him with a daughter, her name would be 'Sophie'. And so it was. And as the tens of thousands of fans cheered and screamed and painted their faces and reached out to touch the larger than life figure they worshipped and idolized - - little Sophie stood at the side of the stage to meet her father when the show was over. Her little fingers clutched his giant hand as they walked together. "You were really good, Daddy."

And that's what he was. Her father. That's what she needed. A Dad. Not an actor or a singer to idolize. But a Father. And so he was.

And he finally understood.

'Just Dad' was an exclusive title; an affirmation of the genuineness and glorious normalcy of their relationship.

To the rest of the world he was the God of Thunder, but only one little girl could call him 'Daddy'.

"I'm not sure when I realized there was a "Holocaust," or even heard the word. They certainly weren't teaching it in Virginia schools back in the 1980s. Eventually, in the 1990s, of course, I heard of it, and about it. Again though, not in school. But it was almost impossible to wrap my mind around the concept, the *reality*, of more than 6 million innocent people killed – ***exterminated*** – in a war that happened more than 30 years before I was born. Then, in 1995, The Holocaust Museum, in Washington, D.C., opened their doors. And opened my eyes. I went with a decent-sized group of people to visit it. We each got a card upon entering. A card with the name and age of a person who had been imprisoned in a German concentration camp. After touring the museum – a sobering and haunting, yet educational experience – there was a list with the names of the people whose cards one received upon entering. Everyone I went with, including myself, "their person" on the card died. Some of these were young children. And as for the displays in museum, there was one I will never forget, never be able to erase from my mind – on either side of a glass bridge that took you from one room in the museum to another, were massive piles of shoes. Burnt black shoes. Charred shoes, many of them so small, they had to have been children's shoes. That's when I finally understood the magnitude, the atrocity, the sheer lingering horror of The Holocaust. I'm still haunted. And sometimes I still have nightmares about those shoes."

-Christopher Beardsley
Co-Administrator: The Flora Army Facebook Site

passover

The sun was beginning to set and Flora readied the table for her invited guests. Soon her darling son would arrive to lead the service and tell the story. With great care, Flora layed out the seder plate; each item specifically placed – symbolizing the ancient struggles of the Jewish people living as slaves under Pharoah's rule.

A roasted egg hardened under the application of heat like the toughened Jewish people despite their grievous suffering.

Haroset like the mortar used to lay bricks for Pharoah.

Maror to remind of the bitterness of slavery.

Salt water like the tears of Hebrews oppressed, with parsley dipped to sharpen its flavor.

A shank bone of the paschal lamb slaughtered like so many innocent Jews throughout history.

And as day became night, Gene – as the man of the house – sat at the head of the table with his yarmulke and haggadah and began to tell the story. He told the story the way millions of others told the story that same night in every imaginable corner of the world. It was the story that Jesus told to his disciples on that final night. That solemn, final night. It was required. The book of Exodus commands it. It commands the Jews to remember God's saving acts and so the story is told again and again: beginning with degradation and concluding with glory and redemption.

It seems impossible. But even in the Nazi death camps, prisoners found ways to tell the story.

Impossible.

The notion of obtaining even a single required ingredient for a seder in the death camps.

But some did. Some held on.

Physically.

Psychologically.

Spiritually.

A reason perhaps to live through the Nazi hell. To survive. To tell the story. To bear witness. To celebrate the exodus from Egypt and, God willing, an exodus from Germany.

First things first. They needed to create or find their own matzah.

Life itself was risked in the pursuit. Often stolen from Camp kitchen cellars. Sometimes bartered for with teeth attached to gold -- small amounts of flour were collected and baked. Cooked on small iron stoves to create burnt, porous wafers vaguely impersonating matzahs.

Matzah.

Often the only ingredient present by which to conduct the seder; though some allowed for the bitterness of their lives to symbolize maror. With luck, the Almighty would understand.

The matzah was divided.

The 'Four Questions' were asked by the youngest

of the group.

The Afikomen went unhidden as there no children left in the camps.

They had all been sent to Auschwitz to be gassed.

The seder proceeded.

Conducted by memory.

Fragments of memory. A Passover collage. A battered, ragtag, disjointed collage they hoped would be enough. Enough to move God to once again deliver them from those who rose up in every generation to destroy them.

Half starved and barely able to move, they prayed. Some praised God. Some asked for favors. Some asked Him to forgive such a poor Passover service. It was the best they could do, they reminded the Lord. They hoped He would hear their prayer and that their exodus from Germany would come soon. Six million died. Six million human beings shot and gassed and hung and burned and electrocuted and tortured by lunatic doctors performing half-assed medical experiments on babies.

Six million died.

Others, by the grace of God, survived.

Survived to tell the story.

Survived to make the exodus.

Survived to bear witness.

The will to bear witness propelling survival in the midst of extremity. Survival allowing eyewitness to atrocity. Survival allowing assurance to the world that goodness remains even in the shadow of great evil. And so the listeners come to hear the testimony of the tellers who survived to bear witness. Surviving voices who take us through the journey from degradation to redemption and freedom. The prisoners were liberated by God and by Man. The slaves were now free. Free to return. But what to return to? What would await? Family members who were already dead? Businesses looted and burned to the ground? Neighbors who'd cheered as they boarded the cattle cars?

Flora returned to her childhood home to find it filled with strangers. She introduced herself, explaining the residence had belonged to her parents. The strangers turned hostile. "We thought Hitler exterminated you rats! This is *our* property now, Jew! Get out of our sight or we'll beat you to pulp and burn you alive!"

Flora found a new home in a Zionist Youth Group. It is where she met Yechiel. The man she would marry. They laughed and loved and hoped and trusted. They planned a life together. And dreamed of Zionism. Of a Jewish homeland. A Jewish State. Was it the only redeemer? The only bearable result? The only imaginable good to come in the wake of the darkest period in all of history? Flora and Yechiel left for Palestine to begin anew. And planned and dreamed and hoped and trusted.

"Even today there are places in Germany where people try to make folks believe that everything was just fine between 1939 and 1945."

-Mike Stone
German Producer, Songwriter, Singer, Guitarist:
'Mike Stone Band', 'The Torpedo Girls',
'Rocket Ride'

"When I was in Germany playing guitar with 'Meatloaf' in the 80's, there was a German label Representative who took us around after one of our concerts and we kind of hit it off. He was a cool guy - we had a blast - and he really took care of us. Sadly, when he dropped me off at our hotel - he made a remark to me that stories of the Holocaust were greatly exaggerated and that most of what was said about it was false. I remember how upset I got. I said nothing because I didn't know what to say. Less than 40 years had gone by and history was already being modified and re-written."

-Bob Kulick
Guitarist on KISS "Alive II"
album, "Paul Stanley" 1978 Solo Album, KISS
"Killers" album, and Paul Stanley 1989 solo tour

the germans make the best ones

Television host Tom Snyder was a strange cross between Ed Sullivan and Richard Nixon -- complete with awkward body movements, hunched posture, stiff speech pattern, piercing eyes, drooping jowls, and a most uncomfortable-sounding laugh best described as a terse series of huffing noises. As a middle-aged man with thick comb-over hairstyle, fancy polyester sports coats, and a stern fatherly presence -- Snyder seemed an odd choice to make a splash on late-night television interviewing rock and roll stars. But he had done just that; interviewing the likes of John Lennon, Patti Smith, Paul McCartney, Johnny Rotten, The Clash and, on Halloween night 1979: the four members of KISS.

For what turned out to be a strange public display of band disunity, Gene sat through the whole of the interview brooding; disgusted with Ace and Peter for being inebriated and unruly on the air. Paul, seated in the middle, appeared nervous and torn between laughing at Ace's drunken antics and remaining serious, professional, and sensitive to Gene in his agitated state. Simmons appeared glum as Ace talked joyfully about getting high on the road, destroying hotel rooms, and throwing remnants of broken property from high-rise balconies onto cars down below on the freeways. This was not the image that Gene wanted to project as KISS was beginning to attract a much younger audience at this phase of their career.

With Snyder egging him on, Ace cackled his way

through story after story: "I'm into radio-controlled model airplanes -- most recently, helicopters....which is more fascinating because they're more challenging. Anyone that's into radio-controlled models knows that right now helicopters are hard to control -- it's a state of the art now. The Germans make the best ones at the moment. Right now I have a Japanese one I'm having trouble with. I have a German one on order."

With that concluding statement about the Germans, Ace began to slowly raise his arm in a Nazi salute.

"Don't do it", Gene growled.

Ace was feeling high, enjoying himself, laughing, and doing his darndest to make great television.

Gene turned sadly towards the camera and quipped, "Hi Mom."

The Germans Make The Best Ones

The context in which the remark was made and the corresponding hand salute were insensitive: but the words were quite true. The Germans, by and large, *did* make the best ones.

Which *ones* are we talking about exactly? Nearly any *one* you can think of.

Symphonies. Time pieces. Architecture. Machinery. Academic Centers. Wines and cuisine. These were people of precision, discipline, accuracy, and detail.

In the context of good, these cultural traits were admirable.

In the context of evil, these cultural traits were incomprehensibly monstrous.

No 'i' went undotted. No 't' uncrossed. The Germans constructed a system of murder so efficient it put the average corporate assemblyline to shame.

No detail was too small to note. Nothing went to waste. Pillows and mattresses were stuffed with human hair. Lampshades were made from human skin. Human fat was rendered into bars of soap. Metal drums were filled to capacity with prosthetic limbs, glass eyeballs, false teeth, and metal-framed spectacles. Nothing slipped through the cracks.

The soldiers photographed it all. Sometimes on the sly against orders – but it was worth it. Merry hunters posing proudly with their slaughtered prey. Photographic trophies. The kind of souvenirs that allow men to relive the glory years of their lives at a later date. Serial killers throughout time have always treasured 'the souvenir': some tangible proof of the deeds that have filled them with such pride. And so the Nazis filmed it all.

The men and the woman. Naked. Humiliated. Freezing. Starving.

The dead. Stacked like piles of wood. Decapitated heads. Collected like balls of yarn in wicker baskets.

SS Doctors. Burning the hands and feet of prisoners with phosphorus.

Amputating limbs and mutilating children. The starving. So hungry they attempt to eat the dressings on their wounds.

Lifeless bodies swing from gallows. Victims. Eyes wide open. Staring in death. Fixed frozen stares that watch us while we cannot believe our eyes. And the construction mining machinery. Pushing mountains of bodies into pits.

Sweet desserts and cakes.
The Germans make the best ones.

Factories of death.
The Germans make the best ones.

And yet – let us not overlook the advantages and rewards of teamwork.
Italy.
Japan.
Hungary.
Romania.
Bulgaria.
Yugoslavia.
Finland.
Iraq.
Thailand.
They all shared a dream. When the dream was shattered, the merciless begged for mercy:
"We were cogs in a wheel and were not privy to Hitler's larger plan."
"We were simply following orders."
Suddenly, everyone -- average citizens and

soldiers alike -- declared their innocence and proclaimed their ignorance.

"We were just regular townsfolk. We didn't know anyone was harming those poor Jews."

"We were just following orders. As soldiers, we had no choice. They would have killed *us* in the gas chambers had we defied our commanding officers."

Declarations. From average citizens and soldiers alike. Cacophonous declarations of innocence and ignorance. Liars and thieves and cowards and murderers. Chanting their mantra: *"We had to follow orders."*

But we know better.

From the very people of precision and discipline and accuracy and detail, we know better.

We know that townsfolk reduced the Jews to pulp with crowbars in broad daylight while crowds gathered and cheered them on. Mothers held their babies and watched happily alongside soldiers who snapped photos and encouraged the violence. When the final skull was smashed like a raw egg, the citizens sang and danced atop the fresh corpses – further pulverizing the brain matter that stuck to their boots as they celebrated.

The murder of Jews in the city streets increasingly became a form of popular entertainment. Police vehicles equipped with megaphones drove through towns announcing when and where the next public execution would take place. Some civilians participated in the beatings and killings while others preferred to stake out prized vantage points such as rooftops and platforms for optimal viewing pleasure.

And what of the soldiers? What of the soldiers who surely would themselves had been killed if they had refused their orders to eliminate the Jewish people?

"We had no choice."

That's what they claimed after the war was over. But we know better.

We know from official written orders, countless testimony, diary entries, and letters mailed home to loved ones that this claim is a myth. <u>The Nazis were forced to obey orders</u> is a myth. An excuse. A denial. A lie.

From the mouths and from the written words of Camp Commandants, Gunmen, Soldiers, Doctors, Inspectors, Engineers, Customs Officials, Chaplains, Gas Van Drivers, Police, Secret Police, Security Police, Auxiliary Police, and Police Reservists: there were no negative consequences whatsoever to an individual who refused to kill Jews. No disciplinary measures. No Court-Martial proceedings. Nothing. If a Soldier refused to commit murder against defenseless people as a part of his job -- he would be reassigned or sent home for psychological and physical rest. In fact, as ruthless as the Nazis were to their enemies, they were quite compassionate toward one another. High-ranking Nazi Heinrich Himmler went so far as to set up a convalescent home in Berlin for soldiers who had suffered psychological breakdowns after killing Jews. He also created an official order in writing stating that men who were unable to deal with the psychological stresses of their jobs would be released from their current duties and sent back home.

Nazi officers were endlessly refining the killing process in order to make the task less unpleasant for their underlings. Members of firing squads did not appreciate the mess associated with having their faces sprayed with the spattered brains of their victims. Something needed to be done to spare the Soldiers this inconvenience. It was decided that Gas-Vans would be used to affixiate victims on the drive over to the mass graves that awaited them. It seemed a splendid idea on paper, but the Soldiers didn't care for the sounds of prisoners screaming and pleading for their lives and soon grew tired of having to unload and clean the interiors of the vehicles as the gassings caused the victims to vomit and empty their bowels. Again, there had to be a way to better reduce the irritations and annoyances associated with the torturing and killing of others. The Nazis thought long and hard. Perhaps large 'shower facilities' filled with Zyklon B……

As the Allies closed in at the end of the war, the Nazis attempted to destroy all physical evidence of their killing machines. They wanted to deny their gas chambers and their ovens. They wanted to deny their medical experimentation on children. They wanted to deny their attempt to completely obliterate an entire race of people from the face of the Earth.

They wanted to deny that the Holocaust had ever occurred at all.

But we know better.

"At first glance, it might be a fascist rally: The giant logo with its prominent and provocative 'SS' all aglow; a man in uniform shouting emphatically; a crowd of thousands with their hands upraised. Then you get a closer look. The crowd is the world, their leader is a Jewish immigrant, and he is telling them "Stand up! You don't have to be afraid!" And there's Flora, singing along. Is this fascism? No. Is it Tikkun Olam ['*repairing the world*']? Maybe. History... or KISStory... will decide!"

-Gary Shaller
Co-Founder: The PodKISSt

"We had festival seating back then, so you could stand right up at the front of the stage. There was the searing heat from the flames, getting spattered with blood and you could almost stick your head in the PA stacks. It was like a horrible industrial accident you *wanted* to be in."

-Jay Evans
Co-Founder:
The KISS Army

the writhing surface of the ocean's skin

The push and pull of swirling humanity mimicked a raging sea as it snapped and lurched from front to back and side to side; wrapping and coiling itself around the edges of the arena to envelop and constrict the teeming swarm of bodies trapped within. The painted warrior shot flames into the air, touching off a frenzy of excitement and activity amongst the assembled collection of eager witnesses as a ripple effect of arms and heads and hands and shoulders overtook the crowd; bouncing and flailing like a thousand buoys bobbing on the writhing surface of the ocean's skin. Swelling and twisting, the larger mass pounded the lone fragments into submission and moved to swallow them whole - swaying hypnotically and solidifying into a single frenetic organism. Readying to mow down any stray remnants of individuality, the human wave stopped at the feet of an older, balding gentleman wearing a jacket and tie. Holocaust survivor Eli Lubowski stood in the eye of this nefarious storm with fingers jammed deep inside his ears and a frozen expression of discomfort plastered on his face. The crowd was roaring in unison and he prayed they weren't chanting 'Sieg Heil'. As his legs began to buckle from the sheer unpleasantness of it all, his new bride -- a jubilant middle-aged woman with heavy Hungarian accent - laughed with joy; jumping up and down and screaming proudly and victoriously in every direction: "That is mine son! That is mine son!"

"While KISS have been accused by many of following trends and bandwagon jumping, they can never be accused of playing it safe. On the heels of their forays into pop/rock territory came '(Music From) The Elder' - a concept album which saw the band accelerate away from their more well-known stomp-along material at warp speed. While some members of the Kiss Army were horrified, others - of which I am one - were thrilled. This was the sound of a band which was not afraid to stretch, experiment, and effectively re-write their own rule-book. This was the sound of a real band."

-Ian Dewar
Member: The KISSFaq

"(Music From) The Elder has a certain charm that is lost on the casual KISS fan, but the diehards have always appreciated the glimpse into the deeper artistic side of the band."

-J. Winkler
Member: The KISSFaq

"The Elder album is a masterpiece. It's like the musical autobiography of Gene Simmons."

-David Sousna
Member: The Flora Army

the elder

Although he deliberately finished his cigarette before entering the conference room, the final waft of cancerous vapor nonetheless settled onto the surface of his tweed jacket; nestling deep within the porous mazes and interlocking colonies of twill-weave. Grunting in vague recognition of the others, the man sat down beside a college boy in seersucker suit. The newbie used aftershave to mask the smell of mothballs and the room took on a mutated odor of stale cigarettes and Aqua Velva. Shooting the men an accusatory glance, a female Associate in purple polyester made a face and turned away -- using her nonverbal skills to announce that something smelled and she didn't like it. Producer Bob Ezrin entered the room to a slight buzz of recognition. Papers were shuffled and pens were clicked. Employees entered and exited again. Some took last minute bathroom breaks returning to find that their seats had been taken. Some arrived late and assumed standing positions in the back of the room.

Reminiscent of the hush that grips a grade school classroom upon the occasion of a visiting Principal, the staff members jolted into a state of exaggerated deference as KISS Manager Bill Aucoin made his way into the proceedings. He was greeted by a sea of frozen smiles and an awkward smattering of scattered applause. Aucoin Management had seen better days. Jobs had been slashed and morale was low. It had been a mere three years but seemed a lifetime ago since the perks and excesses that accompanied KISS' zenith of popularity in 1978. The band and their manager had been to the mountain. They had stood at the top and gazed down upon the pretenders. They owned that mountain. It had been theirs for many years. But as the 70's gave way to the 80's, they found themselves coming down the other side. They needed to re-establish and re-define themselves. They needed to prove that they weren't just a leftover phenomenon from a past decade.

They needed a hit record.

Gene Simmons had an idea.

An idea for a book, to be precise.

The concept had been cooking in his brain for quite some time. Bouncing off his synapse tubes and flowing through his cortex juice.

Setting: a post-apocalyptic world nearly destroyed by a holocaust

Protagonist: a young boy in a strange land

Pattern of Events: an unlikely hero, trained and championed by a wise parental figure, defies the forces of evil to become an embodiment of strength and survival

This was an autobiography.

Cloaked in tights and cape.

Framed in graphic panel form.

Hatched in a Fortress of Solitude.

Perhaps it was a rock album. A concept piece containing spiritual edification and guitar distortion.

Or maybe a narrative Greek Chorus accompanying a fantasy feature film.

Either way, it was Gene, Flora, the Holocaust, and Hitler under assumed names and obscured locations. Gene got down to work, sketching out a rough storyline centered around an ancient sect of immortal, energy-based beings guiding and observing the human race. These overseers – known as The Council of the Elder – interfered not with human choice but, rather mystically steered their subjects and challenged them to be true to their instincts.

Eyes growing heavy, Gene scribbled one last line before surrendering to slumber with pen in hand. He began to ebb and flow upon a sea of shimmering theta waves and locked into a calibrated groove of weightless tones descending.

Straining his ears to see the sights
and losing his grip to find his footing
he held his breath and breathed a sigh
of melody his brain ignited
storyline and song collided
multiplied and subdivided.
And suddenly
Awake.
Awake and so aware of its arrival.
In a dream; a gift in finished state.
The songs poured out from the echoes of his dreams.
Songs about worlds that are lost without heroes.
Songs about answers and questions to find.

Songs about loss and surrendering to darkness.
Songs about faith and belief in oneself.
Songs about seeking the signs of a savior.
Songs about ancient society oaths
where boys become men
and dark becomes light
where weak become strong
and the ordinary grow to be extraordinary.

The dream was a big one and included employing the services of renowned rock producer Bob Ezrin - responsible for the concept album masterworks of Pink Floyd and Alice Cooper. Stage and screen actors were hired to provide dialogue and narratives between songs. The American Symphony Orchestra and St. Robert's Choir were utilized to highlight and accent the fantasy and majesty of Gene's vision. Famed Art Directors David Spindell and Dennis Wolloch produced stunning graphics and dramatic gatefold designs effectively depicting and reflecting the dark medieval themes present in the story.

The last figure to enter the crowded listening space that afternoon was Gene Simmons. Some staffers recognized the man sans Bat-Lizard make-up – but he mostly went unnoticed as he leaned against a wall, folded his arms across his chest, and flashed a broad grin at Manager Bill Aucoin. Bill nodded knowingly at Gene, rose from his chair, and waved the palms of his hands to signal for quiet. Aucoin explained to the group that what they would be hearing today was the first album in an intended trilogy of KISS records documenting the mystical journey of a young boy battling a variety of forces from within and without, ultimately realizing that he had it within his grasp to be a hero all along. The last album of the series would be released simultaneously with a full-length film featuring music from all three records. The scope of the project would be unprecedented, Bill explained, and would occupy the band's creative efforts well into the new decade. With that, Aucoin returned to his seat, the lights dimmed, and the music began. The staffers studied their Press Kits curiously as a medieval fanfare began to seep through the mounted wall speaker system. From the initial violin strains conjuring images of the Klezmer musicians of his youth tuning their instruments in the desert sun through to the concluding words Gene had always hoped to hear his absent father speak to *him*, Simmons was left speechless and trembling with emotion. He exited the room discretely and walked along the winding hallway in a trance of sorts; aware now that he had just re-experienced every sacred, defining, and monumental event in his life in this little room on this average day through the medium of sound and the miracle of art.

This music was a celebration of everything that had ever mattered to Gene. That had ever motivated him. That ever held a single ounce of value in his life.

He had just bared his soul in a way that he perhaps had never done before. To a group of virtual strangers. Assembled in a modest, non-descript room. Where the music had now faded and was replaced by silence. Excrutiating silence. The sort that inspires dread and causes individuals to shift awkwardly in their chairs and release fake coughing sounds. The newbie in the seersucker suit scribbled 'milk' on his notepad as a reminder for the drive home. Bill Aucoin's eyes desperately searched the room for opinions from a sea of faces intent on avoiding his gaze. Papers were shuffled and pens were clicked.

Aucoin grew impatient.

"Okay. Opinion time -- let's go."

"That was KISS?"

"Yes, it was KISS. What did you **think**?"

*"Wow, that **really** didn't sound like KISS...."*

"Trust me, you just heard the new KISS album. Now what did you **think**?"

"Why all the talking in between songs?"

"To keep the story moving."

"Why isn't KISS on the album cover?"

"Gene wanted the music to do all the talking."

"Then why all the talking?"

"To keep the story moving."

*"What **was** the story?"*

"Review your Press Kit, please."

"Why would a KISS fan buy a KISS album that doesn't sound like KISS?"

"We feel confident that the band's fanbase will enthusiastically embrace a broadening of its musical scope."

*And there isn't a picture of KISS **anywhere** on the album? Not even their **logo**?"*

"The music does all the talking."

*" I didn't **like** the talking."*

"It works in tandem with the music."

"I notice the music didn't really sound like KISS...."

"Well, I thank you for your questions, feedback,

and concerns and ask that you keep an open mind as the band enters this new and important phase of their career. Good day."

Aucoin returned to his office and closed the door behind him. He felt confident in having answered all the questions he had already anticipated would be asked of him by his org chart of drones. He forwarded his thoughts and recommendations to the record company, confident that they would recognize "(Music From) The Elder" as KISS' "Sgt. Pepper's".

In the quiet of his apartment, Gene worked enthusiastically on stage set designs, costume prototypes, and some rough song ideas for part two of the trilogy.

In the meantime, the record company decision-makers didn't squirm silently in their chairs, click their pens, emit nervous coughing sounds, or scribble 'milk' on their notepads. They didn't ponder the possibilities of a new stage show and costumes to tie in with the new album. They didn't spend one precious moment thinking of a second or third record in some supposed trilogy. They hated what they heard and took immediate action. First order of business: cut out all but one passage of narration from the album. Next, they re-sequenced the songs so that the harder tunes alternated with the softer ones - storyline be damned. Finally, it may have been too late and too costly to re-do the cover art -- but they would be

Goddamned if the KISS logo wasn't going to be emblazoned on that album cover.

The Gods at Polygram Records had spoken. It was bad enough that they were $220 million in the hole thanks to a poorly calculated takeover of KISS' original Casablanca label. It was cruel enough timing that the music industry in the 80's began losing millions in the wake of counterfeit albums and rampant practices of at-home taping. And it was embarrassing enough that Polygram's business roots had recently been exposed and traced back to Nazi monies and corporations. But *this*.......*this* was too much. This had not been part of the plan; a plan that had revolved around acquiring a tried and proven rock band that would deliver heavy metal music to hordes of heavy metal music fans. The plan had been to make untold millions of dollars on KISS albums and corresponding merchandise. Now the plan was to take back the reigns and slice and dice the record into something that might hopefully resemble a KISS album.

Gene was disgusted by the butchering of his art. Polygram felt duped and halted all support of the record.

KISS fans were confused by the non-linear storyline contained in the final product and spurned the entire venture. In the end – KISS lost fans, Polygram lost money, tour plans were scrapped, future installments of the Elder story were put on permanent hold, and all talk of a motion picture ceased completely.

As depicted in the 1925 film he adored so as a

child, the Phantom's mask had been snatched from his face - - only this time, the mask had been removed by the protagonist's own hand…..and the gesture had likewise been met with gasps of disbelief and cries of derision. All that he was and all he had been hiding - his name, his country, his mother, his religion - had evoked disgust, apathy, and rejection. And, perhaps most painfully, ridicule.

Had the mask that once promised the freedom of an alter-ego and a new identity evolved into a compulsory device for storing secrecy and shame?

Gene had effectively written 'A Day In The Life'. The fans wanted 'She Loves You'. So for the first time in his career, Gene looked outside of KISS for an outlet to grow as an artist. He explored the world of acting and moviemaking to satisfy his ever present need to experience the world of fantasy and the freedom of alter-egos.

In ten years time, the KISS Army would grow to cherish and embrace "(Music From) The Elder"; in the meantime, Gene - exposed and vulnerable - set about re-building the wall…..delving particularly deep into his macabre creation for the next album and tour; his armor especially thick and impenetrable for the occasion.

Gene Simmons

"Having just lost my mother, I can only imagine Gene's love for Flora and his need to take care of her after all she's been through in her life."
-Mike Campion
Gene Simmons Tribute Artist: "Gene's Addiction"

"The lessons of the Holocaust should be mandatory reading for all students to understand the inhuman behavior by Mankind . In order for society to live on in the future, we cannot forget the past - and, hopefully, this generation and generations to come will learn from those horrors that decency, understanding, respect for humanity, and tolerance are the only ways we all can survive in a civil world."
-Carol Ross-Durborow
Personal Manager & Media and Marketing: Aura Entertainment, Inc.
KISS Public Relations – Aucoin Management

"I lost my grandfather in WWII. It was a terrible time in history that must never be forgotten. Flora Klein must be an incredibly strong woman. After all that she went through - she managed to raise a wonderful, brilliant man....May god bless..."
-Joseph Fatale
Member: "Mini KISS"

in flight

Her decision to conclude the trip with a visit to the Yad Vashem Museum left the airline passenger both physically and mentally exhausted. For many days, she had averaged but a few hours of sleep per night and was in dire need of slumber. She closed her eyes and struggled to clear her mind as the aircraft sailed through the clouds of Jerusalem. Drifting in and out of sleep, she shifted in her chair and struggled to find a comfortable position for her feet. Each time that gentle haze of rest enveloped her, she was awakened by an image of the traffic that awaited her outside of LaGuardia. Or the notion of having to make sense of her handwritten notes on Monday. Or the chore of unpacking suitcases and retrieving mail. But mostly, her efforts to sleep were thwarted by that very strange feeling of somebody watching you, even as your eyes are closed. Shifting to her side and exhaling deeply, she opened one eye to find an elderly woman with a warm smile leaning forward no more than two inches from her nose. "My name is Florence. What is your career?" The woman leaned her head back and struggled to reconnect with a state of consciousness. She rubbed her eyes, stifled a yawn, and began: "Well, I'm a full-time wife and mother and that's a job in itself…" Flora listened attentively, nodding her head in agreement. "I'm also a writer. I've got a little blog on my website with a small group of active readers." Flora sipped from a cup and signaled with her eyes for the woman to continue. "A lot of what I focus on is documenting Holocaust survivors. The stories of survivors." At this, Flora's beaming smile momentarily faded and then returned as she quickly changed the topic: "Mine son is famous. Maybe you know of him?" Flora's eyes twinkled as she reached into her purse to retrieve a photograph. "Oh my. Your son is Gene *Simmons*?" "Yes – he is mine son! You know of him? His fame is **very** great."

And Flora's excitement grew as she told her traveling neighbor how wonderful and generous her son was, having just paid for her trip to a spa by the Dead Sea.

Then Flora stopped. She looked carefully to her left and to her right. Her expression grew serious as she whispered, "I was not from Israel, originally. I was born in Hungary. I am a Holocaust survivor." As she spoke these words, Flora looked slowly and suspiciously in each direction – as if revealing her status as a survivor carried with it a smattering of guilt and shame. The woman asked gently, "Have you ever committed your memories and experiences to paper so that others can learn from this awful tragedy?" Flora thought for a moment and then spoke: "No. Unlocking that door would cause me to go mad and I would never come back." Flora turned toward the window. She began to recall the first time El Al had transported her from the Holy Land to New York. It was a journey that she had made with her boy, Chaim, who had been very ill on the plane and had vomited repeatedly. Whether the child was reacting to the uneven motion of the aircraft, the anxiety of leaving behind a beloved homeland, or the traumatic realization that his father was now gone from his life forever - Flora couldn't be sure; but the boy's health had taken a turn for the worse.

"He still throws up", said Flora, "but now his music fans pay him money to do that from on the stage." The woman chuckled softly, moved by Flora's obvious pride and affection for her only son. "Chaim was already feeling ill that morning and that could have been a very real problem."

Mother and child held hands and huddled close inside the cavernous Embassy in Israel that cold December morning in 1958. The elaborate complex of Registry Rooms, staircases, narrow aisles, and tight compartments left Flora feeling positively dizzy. Approaching the Medical Inspector, Flora glanced down nervously at her son's increasingly pale complexion; aware that the doctor could recommend temporary rejection or even permanent exclusion of citizenship if the child be deemed ill and too advanced in his symptoms to recover. Flora and Chaim were instructed to walk slowly and to keep ten feet apart as the doctor took note of his subjects' posture, gait, condition of face, hands, skin, and scalp. Eyelids were everted and checked for contagious granulations. Flora shuttered as her boy was poked, prodded, questioned, and examined for mental and physical defects. The doctor worked quickly and precisely; removing the child's hat, scarf, and collar to ensure they did not cleverly serve to hide goiters, fungus, or deformities. Flora closed her eyes tightly and fought back an intruding memory of young people streaming into the Camp - a meandering line of children limping and crouching; 'undesirables' for German doctors to use for medical research and experiments.

"How old is the boy?" was the question that startled Flora back into the present.

She struggled to recall the best answer to such a question. When the trains would arrive, she remembered boys of 12 claiming to be 16 and men of 50 stating their age as 42. Her Chaim was tall like his father. Surely he could pass for 12 or even 13. Yes, her son was thirteen and would certainly not be a burden in any way. Quite the contrary. He was a solid thirteen and could undoubtedly work as hard as any grown man. Maybe two. Yes. Without a doubt. At the age of thirteen, Chaim was in the prime of his life. Old enough to accomplish the work of two grown men yet young enough to have the kind of motivation and stamina that those two men could only dream of having. It was settled then. Flora had never been more proud of her thirteen year old son.

"Ah, I see here that he'll be nine in August". The doctor scribbled in his notepad, filed their documents in a drawer, placed two identification cards into Flora's hand, and directed mother and child to the main floor of the Registry Room for further processing and inspection. Flora studied the numbers and symbols on her card and they filled her mind with the yellow stars and tattooed limbs of her recent past.

And she trembled.

For a moment she trembled as she watched the congested herd of people lined up in queues twisting this way and that. The noise and the smells and the close proximity threatened to strangle her. More questions followed: Age....occupation......nationality......last residence.... She watched young Chaim shivering and perspiring from fever. *Oh God, they'll never let us cross.* An Examiner Clerk approached. Flora was informed that, as an unaccompanied woman with child, she was required to provide proof that a responsible male family member awaited her. She bit on her lip and listened as her heart pounded in her ears. Beads of sweat fell from Chaim's forehead to the concrete floor.

"Are you now or have you ever been a member of the Communist Party?"

The question was asked in German.

Flora provided her response.

In German.

The language of the Nazis.

"Raise your right hand."

Flora closed her eyes, felt the rumblings of a gag reflex, filled her brain with the words: '*For My Son*', and held her hand straight out in a Nazi salute. Laughing, the Official quickly grabbed Flora's hand and lowered her arm to her side. Their eyes met. He began to laugh once more and then stopped as he recognized her desperate confusion. His face became deadly serious as he leaned in and whispered: "Don't you ever worry, Mrs. Klein. You will never have to do that again. Never again." Flora's eyes welled up with tears as she felt the weight of the universe lifting from her shoulders. "Thank you", she managed to say through choked tears and deep exhalations of relief. "Thank you."

And she bathed in the warm light of profound appreciation. And she dreamed and she reveled in the intoxicating promise of new beginnings. But, most of all, she experienced that very strange feeling of somebody watching you; even as your eyes are closed.

Flora opened one eye to find the woman next to her sipping from a cup and signaling with her eyes for Flora to continue. And as the safety belts were unlatched and the overhead storage compartments were left empty once more, Flora and her new acquaintance walked across the jetway together. "Yours is a very powerful story, Florence. I'd be happy to help you share it with others. Here is my business card." Flora accepted the card but did not read it.

"Do you need a ride home?"

"Oh, thank you darling - but, no. There is a responsible male family member awaiting me", Flora said, smiling mischievously. "I can provide proof." Laughing softly, the woman hugged Flora goodbye and commenced rolling her luggage through the busy airport; fairly certain she had just heard a delighted voice in the distance crying: "My darling son!"

"I believe that many Jewish performers change their names when they enter the entertainment industry due to the unfortunate fact that stereotypes still exist whether we like it or not. These performers, in my opinion, took the mindset that they can appeal to a broader range of people if their ethnic background is less obvious. While there have certainly been strides in regards to overcoming anti-semitism, the stereotypes live on for all races."

-Chris Czynszak
Host: Decibel Geek Podcast

"Jewish entertainers have always taken on gentile-sounding stage names. Jerry Lewis. Joey Ramone. Woody Allen. Cass Elliot. These people wanted to be judged on the basis of their talents; not pre-judged and dismissed by a bunch of anti-semites."

-Gail Schulman
Member: The Flora Army

zimmerman & klein

Singer Robert Zimmerman moved from Minnesota to New York, changed his name to the less Jewish-sounding Bob Dylan, adapted the persona of a Woody Guthrie drifter type, and wrote a batch of songs that altered the face of rock music forever. Singer Chaim Klein moved from Israel to New York, changed his name to the less Jewish-sounding Gene Simmons, adapted the persona of a Bela Lugosi vampire type, and wrote a batch of songs that altered the face of rock music forever.

A decade later, as Gene's devotion to Judaism and shock rock remained solidly in place, Dylan began to flirt with the tenets of Christianity and changed his musical style and lyrical content accordingly. In concert, his audiences were none too pleased with Dylan's latest direction and soon tired of the Jew-turned-Christian's dogmatic preachiness. As irritated members of the crowd called out for Dylan to give the Jesus material a rest and play some rock and roll -- the singer shot back, specifically identifying KISS as the personification of everything evil and unholy about modern music. To a stinging chorus of disapproval, Dylan warned his fans that they could either follow him down the path of righteousness or sink to the pits of hell along with KISS and their heavy metal counterparts.

Interestingly, not only would Dylan later return to Judaism after his 'born again' phase had passed

-- but he also went on to adopt Gene Simmons' use of whiteface make-up in concert on the suggestion of a female band member dating the KISS bassist at the time.

Years passed.

Both men survived the pinnacles and chasms of stardom.

And settled into middle age as musical icons with nothing left to prove.

One afternoon, Gene called Bob and asked if they could write a song together. "Sure thing, Mr. KISS", Dylan replied and the two men spent the day collaborating on guitar chords and melody lines, resulting in the beautiful "Waiting For The Morning Light".

Gene and Bob were pleased with their creation and vowed to work together again.

When reporters expressed shock at the unlikely pairing of the two artists, Gene explained that they were simply a couple of Jewish guys who had long ago taken on gentile names and successfully assimilated into the dominant culture.

As so many had done before them.

As so many will go on to do in the future.

"Gene clearly loves all aspects of fame. It seems he was truly born to be a star."
-Lupe Alvarado-Grod
Member: The Flora Army

"Fanzines were important because they could be written and published by anyone. You didn't have to "break in" or placate an editor. You could just write and publish whatever you wanted, offer to trade copies with people, or send them to other fanzines for reviews. A fan editor could publish his fanzine as long as he wanted to. There was no censorship."
-James Van Hise
Fanzine Historian

"We should always remember the lessons learned from the Holocaust, for it was not only a Jewish tragedy - but also a human tragedy. We should all be more thankful for our freedom and for the power of Rock 'N Roll to bring us all together as one."
-Kevin S. Harp
Musician & Co-founder of "The 1977 CORPS"

smothered and abandoned

At Elmhurst's Newtown High School, the 33rd reunion party for the class of 1968 was well underway. The old gymnasium had been spruced up with balloons, streamers, and crepe paper while the stereo system cranked out tunes like "Kind of a Drag" by the Buckinghams and "To Sir, With Love" by Lulu. Fifty-somethings schmoozed and reminisced, with the majority of the men sucking in their beer bellies while their wives eagerly showed one another photos of their grown children. At Table 17, Sena Rosenberg and Phyllis Mislov studied their old yearbook. "It's too bad our most famous grad never shows up for these things."

"Someone famous went to Newtown?"
"Yeah. Look – next to the photo of Josefa."
"Gene Klein?"
"Yeah."
Sena studied the picture a bit closer. "Who's Gene Klein?"
"That's Gene Simmons. Ya know, that weird Dracula guy from KISS? The rock group? Anyways, that's him. He changed his name."
"Boy, I don't remember a thing about him."
"Me neither. Not a thing. Richie pointed the photo out to me last night. I don't remember him at all. It's like he didn't even exist back then."
"Well, he sure exists *now*. I guess *we're* the ones who don't exist to *him* anymore."

"Who knew this invisible guy would someday become so famous?"

Who knew, indeed.

It's a funny thing.

Fame, that is.

Fame and its magical powers to turn the 'nobody' into the 'somebody'. The way it proves to the world that that individual does, in fact, exist. That the famous individual is legitimate.

He must be. Everybody knows who he is. He is important. Talked about. Photographed. Interviewed. Quoted. Studied. Pursued.

Fame proves to the world that the individual in question matters. And in some cases, it is necessary proof required for the very individual in question. Do I exist? Am I in any way important? Have I impacted the world in any manner at all? Will I live on after my own death and achieve immortality through fame?

Gene's early years in America were marked by his being hassled for standing out as different. As he moved from junior high school through college, he managed to not stand out at all. Being invisible kept him safe from bullies - but devastated his sense of self and awakened his acute need to be noticed and admired. He harnessed small doses of the regard he so desperately craved by winning a dance contest in school, but the majority of his early attempts at wowing an audience left much to be desired. At camp, Gene's first foray into singing was publically cut short when a large moth flew into his mouth and down his throat. At Roosevelt Junior High School, Gene was set to perform with a band of musicians he dubbed "Lynx" -- the image of a wild cat firing his imagination. When the Principal mistakenly introduced the boys as 'The Missing Links' – intimating that they were a group of cavemen - the Administrator unwittingly ridiculed Gene and his bandmates before their peers. After graduating from Richmond College, Gene set out to find a captive audience as a Teacher in Spanish Harlem. He lasted only a few months -- frustrated that his 'audience' did not applaud him at the end of the school day.

And although a perfectly respectable profession, did his mother survive the horrors of the Holocaust for her son to simply teach a roomful of screaming school children? Didn't he owe her more for her suffering? Didn't he need to shake up the world in honor of her survival?

Gene wanted to be famous. And like so many other individuals who later succeed in achieving fame, Gene started out as a Fan. A diehard Fan. A Fan who wrote, illustrated, and published his own Fan Magazines. He envisioned himself a renowned horror movie actor or comic book artist. Perhaps a musician. It didn't really matter. Fame was the goal; the vehicle was less important and yet to be defined. The only desire was to be a person of note. It was an all-consuming singular vision. To make history. To enjoy the spoils of prominence. He had no interest in being a tragic person who died young, achieved celebrity status only in death, or experienced fame briefly in his lifetime only to die as a forgotten figure.

Gene wanted to famous. Iconic. Forever.

On reflection, Gene Simmons was both abandoned and smothered. Either ingredient can lead to a fierce drive for constant adulation. Together, the opposing experiences were combustible and filled Gene with an unquenchable desire for stardom.

"I'll show *them*"

The mantra of the invisible.

A common motivator for seekers of fame.

Seekers who have been both rejected and abandoned by peers and parents alike.

Gene's father abandoned him.

His peers ignored him.

His beloved mother left him alone for inordinate periods of time when forced to take over as the family breadwinner.

Gene was shunned and abandoned because the world did not recognize how special he was. They were wrong. He was special and he would *prove* it. The world would someday know his name and rue its gross misjudgment of his significance.

"You are the most special child. Better and smarter than all the others."

These words would warm his soul and inflate him with possibility.

Mother's words.

Mother's embrace.

The sweetest, warmest, safest glow of love and energy in all the universe.

His mother's soothing and adoring words would envelop him and shroud him in a blanket of glorification bordering on worship. It was the most potent, addicting elixir Gene would ever know and he would seek to replicate the experience for all time.

The attainment of fame would ensure this continued sense of beatification.

There was really only one solution.

He needed to transform the world into the role of audience.

To be looked at. Noticed. Adored. Admired. Envied.

Those who abandoned needed to realize how foolishly they had underestimated him.

Those who believed needed to continue to idolize and exalt him.

It was compulsory.

No matter what it took to get to the top.

It was imperative.

The fame. The glory. The brightest spot on the stage.

The stage and its intoxicating promises of stardom. The stage as a scene of epiphany: *the risk of public humiliation in the spotlight is preferable to the promise of anonymity in the shadows.*

For the chance to discard the past and create a new life, it was worth risking everything.

For the chance to soothe the wounds of exclusion and neglect, it was worth risking everything.

And so he risked everything. And Gene became a star.

And we gave him what he wanted. An endless supply of love and adulation.

And he gave us what we needed. Excitement. Escape. And the illusion of knowing someone far more special than ourselves.

"Israel is the ancient Jewish homeland where Jews have been in residence for over three thousand years. It's the Jewish experience incarnate and every Jew has deep feelings for our ancestral homeland."
-Rabbi Shmuley Boteach

"Will there ever be peace in Israel? Only if the Moshiach comes! Until then…..no peace."
-Rabbi Rachamim Pauli

"My grandfather, who was with the Army Corps of Engineers, took snap shots during the liberation of Buchenwald. I've had people tell me in the past that Buchenwald was a "labor" camp not a "death" camp. These pictures of ovens and stacks of bodies tell quite a different story. They can call these camps whatever they like - but people died in all of them: whether by starvation and disease or gas chamber."
-Leigh Ann Parham
Member: The Flora Army

a return to israel

53 years since he had last sold the sabra cactus fruit, climbed the neighbor's fig tree, seen his father in the arms of another woman, and fallen ill on the plane that whisked him away to America, Gene Simmons came back to Israel. He saw the hospital where he had been born. He visited the café where Flora had worked as a young woman.

He rode a camel through the desert. He held a press conference and spoke in Hebrew. He revealed his birth name and what his mother had experienced in the concentration camps.

He introduced his grown son and marveled at his 6' 7" frame: "Now *that's* a Macabee!" Gene declared with pride and affection. He reminded the gathering of reporters that Israel was sacred ground for Muslims, Jews, and Christians alike. As flash bulbs popped and reporters scribbled in their notepads, Gene explained that prior to coming to America, he had lived with his mother and father in Wadi Ghamal, Tirat Ha Carmel. "I left Israel. But I'm back", Gene proclaimed. "This is home." He appeared both relieved and surprised by his own words.

The following day was marked by a visit to the Yad Vashem Holocaust Museum, located at the foot of Mount Herzl. Swelling with emotion, Gene made his way through the multi-media presentations and personal artifacts of survivors. Camp uniforms. Clothes taken from the gas chambers. The braids of a little girl – cut off by her mother before her death in Auschwitz.

Within the 10 exhibition halls, the displays were set up chronologically. A Master Database contained 3.8 million names of Holocaust victims and over 385,000 photographs. The Oral History Section housed some 101,000 audio, video, and written testimonies. There were exhibitions commemorating non-Jews who risked their lives to save Jews during the Holocaust. There was a Children's Memorial honoring the 1.5 million Jewish children who perished in the camps; complete with the flickering flames of memorial candles reflected in an infinity of tiny lights in the prevailing darkness. Perched on the edge of an abyss, an original cattle car used for transporting victims to death camps was displayed. At the conclusion of the Museum was the Hall of Names - a memorial to the 6 million Jews who perished in the Holocaust.

Emerging from the cavernous structure in tears, Gene approached a balcony where light was visible once more. The view of Jerusalem was spread out before him like an oil painting and each step taken away from the museum provided a swelling impression of safety; a sense of the evil done to Jews being literally and figuratively behind him.

He wished it like a prayer.

But before the dream could reach his brain and

send a signal to process a smile, a bus exploded.
   Off in the distance.
   One dead, forty-seven injured.

"People say you can never *really* go home again. Sometimes I wonder if my memories of childhood have any actual resemblance to the realities of my childhood."

-Phil Josie
Member: The Flora Army

"What Hitler did was wrong and we must always remember the Holocaust. I am so happy that Flora survived and brought her son to live in the freedom of the USA."

-Kevin Warhaft
Host: Kevin Warhaft's KISS Radio Show, Miami Florida

"Although I can never imagine what Flora went through in overcoming the fate of her family, it may seem that her son Gene found his catharsis in a band called KISS by establishing an icon of western pop culture without caring for given regulations or boundaries. When Gene seems to be a restless soul from the outside, it's obvious that his work ethics and perspective to celebrate each day above ground as the last one were clearly driven by his mother and her history. Without Flora Klein - no Gene Simmons - no KISS - no devoted fans - and no piles of books about these four influential guys from New York City."

-Ingo Floren
Author: The "Official Price Guide to KISS Collectibles"

childhood's end

His trip to New York had been anything but a vacation what with two business meetings before lunch, a lunch meeting, a post-lunch press conference, and a pre-dinner business gathering with his 'Simmons Records' partners and associates. Gene took care to stay immutably busy at all times. It had made him a rich man while keeping his thoughts from venturing down alleyways in his brain that stored the most dolorous events from his past. And yet it was the past exactly that he felt drawing him in like a magnet that evening as the cab drove ever closer to the guideposts of his childhood.

The vehicle stopped.

The driver was paid.

The sun fixed to set.

Approaching the aging structure, Gene touched the faded brass doorknob of his youth and moved his hand along the rough wood grain of the old front door. He noticed his fisheye reflection in the rim of the peephole as a series of footsteps grew louder in response to his ringing the bell. Breathing deeply, he waited for his cue. The front door opened like a stage curtain. He was on.

"Hi, my name is Gene. I used to live here when I was a little boy. I hate to trouble you but I'd love to see the place again after all these years. It holds a lot of memories. May I come in for just a little bit?"

And with that, Gene Simmons took a step back in time -- back to the childhood apartment he shared with his mother Flora in the 1960's. To the home where he had learned the guitar and the chordal secrets of his favorite songs by slowing down the speed control on his record player. To the home where he had practiced drawing superheroes and comic strip characters.

To the home where he had kept a diary chronicling his teenage troubles and concerns.

Gene glanced to his left and spotted the location where the black and white family television set once resided -- typically tuned to Channel 9's "Million Dollar Movie" showcasing horror classics like King Kong, Godzilla, and Rodan. This was the room where he had studied Talmud, read about the Holocaust, learned to dance 'The Twist', and had first seen The Beatles perform on 'Ed Sullivan'. It was where he had fantasized about being a Rabbi. And, later on, a Rock Star.

Making his way through the cramped kitchen area, Gene marveled at a tiny nook that once housed his vast collection of Fanzines -- all expressing a fixation and obsession with the strange, the mysterious, the amazing, and the macabre. Not only did Gene write about and illustrate a world of fantasy within those pages -- but he also contributed Editorials and expressed his desire to one day achieve great fame.

In that apartment, Gene composed an impressive

number of songs -- everything from rock and roll to folk music to country and western and everything in between.

In fact -- every interest, passion, fantasy, and dream that Gene would later develop and make real in the future originated in that home. It was where he had invented Gene Simmons.

The house tour ended with the floor plan looping him back around to the front door hallway. Shaking the man's hand, Gene stated: "I never imagined that one day I'd be coming back here. Thank you for the opportunity."

And with that, he stepped out of the one bedroom/ one bathroom unit and onto the street; standing for a time and staring wistfully at the front of the building. "I can't believe how small it is", he said to himself– fighting the lump in his throat. "It used to seem like the whole world."

"Years ago I saw an elderly lady with numbers tattooed on her arm. I asked her if after going through everything she had gone through, did she find herself hating Germans today. She looked me in the eye and said, 'No, you can't hate. Hate is what put those numbers on my arm in the first place.' I will never forget that woman or the lesson she taught me that day."

-John Toes
Member: The Flora Army

"Remembering the Holocaust leaves no better example, and no better reason, for all civilized people to do whatever they have to do to prevent a horror like that from ever happening again - no matter what the cost!"

-Lydia Criss
Author: "Sealed With A KISS"
First Wife of KISS Drummer Peter Criss
Inspiration for the Award-Winning, Classic KISS Song: "Beth"

plenty of time to rest

Gene moved swiftly through the well-traveled streets of the city, walking this way and that - - ever in motion. Juggling the numbers and percentages of his myriad business ventures, the mechanisms in his brain fired with mathematical precision; meandering and moving with measured purpose. Till the edges would blur. Till investment ideas would melt into indistinguishable globs of brainstorming sessions and half-finished marketing strategies. With control and focus diminishing fast, Gene sought to channel a sense of tranquility in the shape of a song. Like a subconscious mumble or muttering of white noise designed to distract the listener from hearing the colors of his deepest insecurities. Like a lilting drone to take the place of an intrusion of competing thoughts and ideas. It was a melody of the author's personal making; with apologies, to be sure, to the regional minor scales that informed him so very many years before. Gene took a deep breath and sorted out the business priorities of the day.

E-mails were sent.

Phone calls were placed.

Messages were left.

Contracts were signed.

There was much to accomplish.

And there was no slowing down.

He would have plenty of time to rest when he was dead.

Besides.......the crowd was waiting.
And although the crowd knew well the routine they were soon to witness – they anticipated it with excitement nonetheless. This was KISS' "Farewell Tour" and the children of the '70's were now middle-aged adults bringing their own children to witness the spectacle.
The leather-clad beast in war paint and dragon boots advanced slowly towards the foot of the stage. The dissonant bass. The paranoid eyeballs. The spurting blood and the serpentine tongue. All the familiar elements were in place and the colony of wild-eyed spectators rushed forward to collect the splattering overflow as they'd done so many times before over the last 38 years. Taking one last look at the glorious mayhem he had created, Gene smiled with a mischievous twinkle in his eyes and made his exit stage right.

Later, away from the dizzying lights and punishing sounds, Gene sat alone in silence and began his ritual of wiping away the blood and the white face and the bat-shaped greasepaint and the sweat that covered his aging face. His hair dyed jet black to conceal his greying locks, he began working make-up remover into the crow's feet around his eyes. Peering deeply into a small round magnified mirror, he caught the reflection of a pair of eyes from behind him.

And he could see the love in those eyes.
For they were the eyes of his mother.

Eyes.

Eyes that brimmed with optimism despite having every reason on Earth to live her remaining years in fear, hate, and sadness.

Eyes.

Eyes that seemed to overflow with survival and forgiveness.

Eyes.

Eyes that he still had so very much to learn from. His mother's eyes.

The sky was dark when Gene arrived back at his hotel room.
He took to the edge of the mattress and removed his socks and shoes.
Listening to the soft lilting drones of his childhood, he rocked his body in fixed gentle intervals as if in prayer.
Picking up the telephone, he placed a call to Flora.
He had accomplished a lot and experienced a great deal.
It had been another good day above ground.
And he had much to tell her.

ACKNOWLEDGMENTS

I would like to thank my mom and dad for giving me life and for always supporting me in my endeavors. My brother for being my best friend and my sister for enduring years and years of KISS music she didn't want to hear. My Grandparents for teaching me where I came from. My Omi for getting us out of Nazi Germany. My friends Robert Barrie and Brian Christopherson for being my best 'KISS Friends' when I was a child. The music of KISS. The music of The Beatles. My dear friends and bandmates Evan Rotman, Brian Tagomori, Doug Shaffer, Matt Podolsky, and Damian Spooner. Early KISS book authors John Swenson, Robert Duncan, and Peggy Tomarkin. Friends and fans I met online at the original KISSAsylum.com, Frehleygirl's Hideaway, KISSonline.com, Paul Stanley's Paradise, The KISS Detention Hall, The KISS Fan Site.com, and my own Almost Human page on Yuku.com. I would like to thank Shannon Tweed for bringing my 'Flora Army' webpage to the attention of her Webmistress Valerie Young. A big thanks to 'Family Jewels' Producer Adam Freeman. I would like to express my appreciation to the 25,000 members of 'The Flora Army' Facebook page and to my dearest Co-Administrators Christopher Beardsley and Adam Nierenberg. Special thanks to my bestest buddy Brian Finck for his treasured friendship and the rest of my 'second family' of co-workers. Thank you to Daniel Levitch for his enthusiasm, feedback, and expertise. Thank you to the talented Amy Jamieson for all of her wonderful feedback on book cover ideas when I was struggling with images and concepts. I would like to thank all of the people who took time out of their busy schedules to supply wonderful and moving quotes for this book. To the following authors who inspired me to want to write a book of my own: Julian Gill, Christopher Lendt, Steven Lee Beeber, Dale Sherman, J. Randy Tarraborelli, Rabbi Simcha Weinstein, and Ms. Carl Friedman - - whose book 'Nightfather' inspired me to not only want to *write*, but to emulate the simple, minimalistic style she so beautifully perfected. Thank you to Hannah Lee and Mark Levine at 'Mill City Press' for their care and professionalism. I want to remind everyone to remember those that the 'KISS Family' has lost: Neil Bogart, Sean Delaney, Seth Dogramajian, Eddie Balandas, Eric Carr, Stan Penridge, Mark St. John, and Bill Aucoin. Mr. Aucoin was one of the first individuals to join my 'Flora Army' Facebook page and took the time to send me a private message of support and encouragement. I will never forget that. I will also be forever grateful to Bill Starkey who founded 'The KISS Army' in the 1970's and who championed me every step of the way as I wrote this book. The same goes for KISS Insider and Author of 'KISS And Sell' Christopher Lendt for his constant encouragement and wise advice throughout. Thank you to Steven Lee Beeber whose amazing book "The Heebie Jeebies at CBGB's: A Secret History of Jewish Punk" gave me a whole new appreciation for Jewish rebellion and for his personal votes of confidence in my project along the way. I am also grateful to Lydia Criss for her warmth and guidance through it all. I want to thank my beautiful wife, my little precious daughter, and my dashingly handsome son for their love and patience with me while I spent so much time researching for – and writing – this book. A shout out to special family and friends: Mike Gruen, Victoria and Jack, Andres – Carol – Sara – Emmy, Jeff - Lily - Daniel, Rauly Curran, Karen Salter, Hector – Ana – Lily, Suegro y Suegra, Robert Gomez, Ruth and Renee, Liron – Diana - Bella – Aaron, Tia Eva and Nadia, Alan Theodore, the Eisenbergs and Rosanne, Jonathan, Rachel and Sara Lehmann. A big hug to Pearl Dogramajian and Raina Marie for their memories of the late great Seth Dogramajian. I would like to thank God for all the blessings in my life. Finally – I would like to thank Gene Simmons for the music, the magic, and the make-believe; I simply don't know how I would have made it this far without the fantasy and escape you still provide me to this day.

And to Flora......you are the embodiment of strength, beauty, courage, and optimism. "The Flora Army" loves and honors you. Thank you for the light you bring to this world.

AFTERWORD

gene is the man of 1,000 faces
a sculptor of wild fantastical dreams
his music takes me to magical places
where everyday life is much more than it seems

the awe and the wonder i felt as a boy
continues to shape all my hopes and my fears
i thank you for letting me share in the joy
of this journey of 1,000 years.

"Flora's life story is an inspiring one, and is so much more personal to us, because we all know her son, one of the Gods of Rock and co-founder of the biggest Hard Rock bands of all time. She is strong, courageous and beautiful, and we can all learn from her example of what it means to never give up on living your life on your own terms."

-Carrie Larsen
The Flora Army

"I am a child survivor of the Holocaust. My wish, hope and prayer is for every child to grow up in peace without hunger and prejudice."

-Inge Auerbacher
Author and Inspirational Speaker

"We must never forget this, the darkest hour in human history. We cannot allow people to downplay what happened or question the reality of it or we will be doomed to repeat it. My wife's grandfather was part of the force that liberated The Wöbbelin camp. His firsthand stories of what he and the other soldiers of the 82nd found there cannot be questioned and must always be remembered, as should the strength and character of those who survived that horrible page in our history."

-Warren Lapine
Editor: The KISS Magazine

"The Holocaust was the most sadistic, horrific, devilish crime that ever existed. I thank God for those who survived and will always remember those who were murdered. It is always inspiring to hear testimony from those who survived. There will always be a place in my heart for them all. I believe if it wasn't for Gene's mom, rock and roll wouldn't be what it is today. God bless."

-Michael Zimmonz
Gene Simmons Tribute Member

"The Holocaust defined evil and born from that evil was the killing of a certain tranquility on earth. There should never be an end to speaking or writing about it because to do so would be for future generations to forget, and forgetting would be another tragedy for humanity. It was a time of infamy we are cursed to remember so that no generation shall ever forget."

-Bryan J. Kinnaird
Author: 'Sean Delaney's Hellbox'

"The killing of millions of Jews and other people by the Nazis during World War II is one of the darkest chapters in human history. The survivors of the Holocaust overcame prejudice, intolerance and bigotry. Those who survived made a difference - they are an example of human spirit, resilience and courage. They suffered what the rest of mankind can only imagine, their stories will continue to inspire generations forever."

-David Snowden
KISS Merchandise/Promotions

"I'll be honest; I knew nothing about the holocaust before 9th grade English class. In fact, I didn't know about Jewish people as a group really (there are no synagogues in my hometown). At the same time though, I was really discovering rock 'n' roll, specifically KISS. It's when you combine all those elements of Gene's childhood; his mother Flora; surviving the Holocaust and their moving to America, it is nothing short of magical that we have the Gene Simmons we do today."

-Norman Huizenga
Founding Member: The KISS Detention Hall Website

"It is our duty to remember the Holocaust not only out of respect for the people who endured it, but also out of love for our fellow Man so that it will never be repeated."

-Valerie Young
Webmistress: The Fans Of
Shannon Tweed Facebook Page

"Gene Simmons and his mother Florence are an inspiration to all of us rock fans. His mom survived the horrors of the Holocaust and brought her son Gene to the USA where he helped create one of greatest rock bands ever. It is the American dream, and at the same time, a lesson that the Holocaust should never be forgotten. Had Florence perished, KISS would never have existed......so NEVER FORGET."

-Terri Bey
Member: The original KISSOnline.com

"Growing up, I was always taught that history should never be forgotten. We can learn by the mistakes and accomplishments of the Human Race. The Holocaust was a terrible time of Jewish oppression. We must continue to learn from the mistakes of that era and make sure it will never happen again."

-Alicia Jurries
Founding Member:
The KISS Detention Hall Website

"Flora Klein serves as an inspiration to everyone in that not only did she survive the horrific Holocaust but instilled in her son positives despite the horror she experienced. Flora represents the best in humanity, in that she has faced unimagineable terror, horror and genocide yet embraced the good in humanity through perserverance, faith and a determination to survive. Whether Jew or Gentile, we must never foget the atrocities that she, and millions of others suffered and experienced at the hand of human monsters. She truly represents the faith in God and the spirit of determination, survival and love and serves as an example and reminder that we, the human race, must grow and prevent such an atrocity from ever happening again. We have a responsibility to teach the new generations. We must never forget."

-Doc Lehman
Journalist

"I believe that remembering the Holocaust is not enough if we want to prevent it. We must teach the victims to heal their souls, and forgiveness will do that. I know that forgiveness is healing, liberating and self-empowering, I have done it. The victims who are healed do not want revenge. I believe and know that anger is a seed for war, forgiveness is a seed for peace, and we all hope for peace."

-Eva Kor
Founder: CANDLES ("Children of Auschwitz Nazi Deadly Lab Experiments Survivors") Holocaust Museum and Education Center

SOURCE NOTES:

The following quotations refer to the chapter sections in *this book* and the reference materials that inspired them; they are not quotes from the reference materials themselves.

"WC" indicates web citations.

"Timeline and Points of Interest"

Dershowitz, Alan. *The Case For Israel*. New Jersey: John Wiley & Sons, Inc., 2003

"Famous Monsters of Filmland" #226, p.21, 1999

Gene Simmons Official Website http://www.genesimmons.com

IMDB: 'KISS: Beyond The Make-Up' http://www.

imdb.com/title/tt0399247/

"KISS Krazy" Fanzine #4, 1984

Leaf, David and Ken Sharp. *KISS – Behind The Mask: The Official Authorized Biography.* New York: Warner Books, 2003.

Lendt, C.K. *KISS And Sell: The Making of a Supergroup.* New York: Billboard Books, 1997.

Simmons, Gene. *KISS And Make-Up.* New York: Three Rivers Press, 2002.

Simmons, Gene. *Sex, Money, KISS.* Beverly Hills: Simmons Books, 2003.

Stanley, Paul and Gene Simmons. *KISSTORY.* Los Angeles: KISSTORY Ltd., 1994

"Traits and Characteristics of Children of the Holocaust"

Epstein, Helen. *Children of the Holocaust: Conversations with Sons and Daughters of Survivors.* New York: Penguin Books, 1988.

Friedman, Carl. *Nightfather.* New York: Persea Books, 1995.

Glassner, Barry and Hillary Taub Lachoff. *The Jewish Role in American Life*. Los Angeles: Casden Institue, 2004.

Hass, Aaron. *In The Shadow of the Holocaust: The Second Generation*. Cambridge: University Press, 2001.

Spiegelman, Art. *Maus*. New York: Pantheon Books, 1986.

Wiesel, Elie. *Night*. New York: Hill & Wang, 1972.

"an x-ray of his own soul"

"The leather clad beast in warpaint and….." Duncan, Robert. *KISS* p. 24. New York: Popular Library, 1978.

"Poster advertisement of a fat man in a red suit….." Simmons, Gene. *KISS And Make-Up* p. 25. New York: Three Rivers Press, 2002.

"The cruel eyes of school children are upon….." 'Gene Simmons on Shrink Rap with Pamela Stephenson',UK: Channel Four. Episode Eight; 28 April 2008.

"This new language is ugly. It is too hard to….."
Simmons, Gene. *KISS And Make-Up* p. 30. New York: Three Rivers Press, 2002.

ADDITIONAL SOURCES

Epstein, Helen. *Children of the Holocaust: Conversations with Sons and Daughters of Survivors*. New York: Penguin Books, 1988.

Hass, Aaron. *In The Shadow of the Holocaust: The Second Generation*. Cambridge: University Press, 2001.

Spiegelman, Art. *Maus*. New York: Pantheon Books, 1986.

"sabras"

"Like cactus fruit. Like a whirling….."
Simmons, Gene. *Sex, Money, KISS* p.23. Beverly Hills: Simmons Books, 2003.

"A lilting drone to take the place of….."
Leaf, David and Ken Sharp. *KISS – Behind The Mask: The Official Authorized Biography* p. 408. New York: Warner Books, 2003.

"Uncle Larry and Aunt Magda were….."

Simmons, Gene. *KISS And Make-Up* p. 27. New York: Three Rivers Press, 2002.

"It was so like America. The whirling….."
'Gene Simmons on Shrink Rap with Pamela Stephenson',UK: Channel Four. Episode Eight; 28 April 2008.

ADDITIONAL SOURCES
Hass, Aaron. *In The Shadow of the Holocaust: The Second Generation*. Cambridge: University Press, 2001.

Spiegelman, Art. *Maus*. New York: Pantheon Books, 1986.

"what was once a banana stalk"

"He remembered it reminded him of maple syrup and….."
WC: http://www.kennhoekstra.com/musings/blood.html

"Climbing that fig tree was difficult work, but….."
'Gene Simmons on Shrink Rap with Pamela Stephenson',UK: Channel Four. Episode Eight; 28 April 2008.

"And so clutching the banana stalk….."

Simmons, Gene. *KISS And Make-Up* p. 18. New York: Three Rivers Press, 2002.

"Arriving into the safety of his mother's arms, she….."
'Gene Simmons on <u>Shrink Rap with Pamela Stephenson</u>',UK: Channel Four. Episode Eight; 28 April 2008.

"The door opened. 'Did you hit my…..'"
York: Three Rivers Press, 2002. Simmons, Gene. *KISS And Make-Up* p. 18. New

"She repeated these words to the Sergeant who looked….."
'Gene Simmons on <u>Shrink Rap with Pamela Stephenson</u>',UK: Channel Four. Episode Eight; 28 April 2008.

"Remember, my son – any day above….."
WC: <u>http://www.genesimmons.com</u>

<u>ADDITIONAL SOURCES</u>
Dachs, David. *Rock's Biggest Ten*. New York: Scholastic Book Services, 1979.

Robinson, Richard. *Rock Revolution*. New York: Popular Library/Creem Magazine, 1976.

"enormously much and overwhelmingly little"

"Flora and Yechiel met and married after…."
Simmons, Gene. *KISS And Make-Up* p. 13. New York: Three Rivers Press, 2002.

"Chaim peered upwards and saw his father. His excitement….."
'Gene Simmons on Shrink Rap with Pamela Stephenson',UK: Channel Four. Episode Eight; 28 April 2008.

"My God, there had been *thousands*. Every size and….."
Lendt, C.K. *KISS And Sell: The Making of a Super-group* p.240. New York: Billboard Books, 1997.

"Control life or it controls….."
Gene Simmons on Shrink Rap with Pamela Stephenson',UK: Channel Four. Episode Eight; 28 April 2008.

ADDITIONAL SOURCES
Gross, Michael Joseph. *Starstruck: When A Fan Gets Close To Fame*. New York: Bloomsbury, 2005

Robinson, Richard. *Rock Revolution*. New York: Popular Library/Creem Magazine, 1976.

"sweet serenading silence"

"The mimeograph flyer read: SEE THE….."
Stanley, Paul and Gene Simmons. *KISSTORY* p. 3.
Los Angeles: KISSTORY Ltd., 1994

"With special care, Gene removed his bass….."
Simmons, Gene. *Sex, Money, KISS* p.31. Beverly Hills: Simmons Books, 2003.

"How they forced him to use his trumpet like….."
WC: http://www.holocaust-lestweforget.com/orchestra.html

"They played all night as the Nazis continued….."
Spiegelman, Art. *Maus* p.50. New York: Pantheon Books, 1986.

"When those in line could no longer stand straight….."
Langer, Lawrence L. *Holocaust Testimonials: The Ruins Of Memory* p. 27. New Haven: Yale University Press, 1991.

"But *mostly,* Vladek remembered….."
WC: http://www.holocaust-lestweforget.com/orchestra.html

"Dr. Mengele would smile and sway and would….."
Jacobs-Altman, Linda. *The Importance of Simon*

Wiesenthal p. 20. New York: Lucent Books, 1999.

"Hi, I'm Seth Dogramajian and….."
Simmons, Gene. *Sex, Money, KISS* p.31. Beverly Hills: Simmons Books, 2003.

ADDITIONAL SOURCES
Bukiet, Melvin Jules. *Nothing Makes You Free: Writings By Descendants of Jewish Holocaust Survivors.* New York: W.W. Norton & Company, Inc., 2002.

"is there room for three?"

"To be an only child. To be an only….."
Simmons, Gene. *KISS And Make-Up* p. 17. New York: Three Rivers Press, 2002.

"Gene Klein spends his days with Stephen….."
Simmons, Gene. *KISS And Make-Up* p. 42. New York: Three Rivers Press, 2002.

"Stephen Coronel and Stanley Eisen. Guitars in….."
Simmons, Gene. *KISS And Make-Up* p. 56. New York: Three Rivers Press, 2002.

"Stanley this is Gene. Gene this is….."
Simmons, Gene. *KISS And Make-Up* p. 57. New York: Three Rivers Press, 2002.

"You think you've got some special aura….."
Simmons, Gene. *KISS And Make-Up* p. 58. New York: Three Rivers Press, 2002.

"Epic Records comes-a-calling with….."
Simmons, Gene. *KISS And Make-Up* p. 61. New York: Three Rivers Press, 2002.

"When you were a child your mother Flora told you….."
Simmons, Gene. *KISS And Make-Up* p. 57. New York: Three Rivers Press, 2002.

ADDITIONAL SOURCES
Gross, Michael Joseph. *Starstruck: When A Fan Gets Close To Fame*. New York: Bloomsbury, 2005.

Tomarkin, Peggy. *KISS: The Real Story*. New York: Dell Publishing, Inc., 1980.

"all relative"

"For every creature that experiences….."
Klee, Ernst. *The Good Old Days: The Holocaust As Seen By Its Perpetrators And Bystanders* p.23. Connecticut: Konecky and Konecky, 1991

"And so the man's time as a soldier during….."
Gebert, Gordon G.G. and Bob McAdams. *KISS & Tell* p. 68. New York: Pitbull Publishing, 1997.

"Frehley seized a pencil, a ruler, and a can….."
Gebert, Gordon G.G. and Bob McAdams. *KISS & Tell* p. 41. New York: Pitbull Publishing, 1997.

"His mind latched onto an image of an impeccably….."
Steinbacher, Sybille. *Auschwitz: A History* pp. 102-103. New York: Harper Collins, 2005.

"MAX'S KANSAS CITY. And there it stood….."
Beeber, Steven Lee. *The Heebie-Jeebies At CBGB's: A Secret History of Jewish Punk* p. 39. Illinois: Chicago Press Review, Inc., 2006.

"Degenerate Jewish art. Kids who…."
Beeber, Steven Lee. *The Heebie-Jeebies At CBGB's: A Secret History of Jewish Punk* p. 8. Illinois: Chicago Press Review, Inc., 2006.

"They took Adolph's beloved symbols of….."
Beeber, Steven Lee. *The Heebie-Jeebies At CBGB's: A Secret History of Jewish Punk* p. 175. Illinois: Chicago Press Review, Inc., 2006.

"Grueling sessions of potent animal-like….."
Beeber, Steven Lee. *The Heebie-Jeebies At CBGB's: A Secret History of Jewish Punk* p. 164. Illinois: Chicago Press Review, Inc., 2006.

ADDITIONAL SOURCES
Bukiet, Melvin Jules. *Nothing Makes You Free: Writings By Descendants of Jewish Holocaust Survivors*. New York: W.W. Norton & Company, Inc., 2002.

Glassner, Barry and Hillary Taub Lachoff. *The Jewish Role in American Life*. Los Angeles: Casden Institue, 2004.

Hass, Aaron. *In The Shadow of the Holocaust: The Second Generation*. Cambridge: University Press, 2001.

"by its very nature"

"Shiny waves of golden brown hair had….."
Swenson, John. *Headliners: KISS* p. 100. New York: Grosset & Dunlap, Inc., 1978.

"For Flora Klein, every hair roll, fingerwave….."
WC: http://hot1940shairstyles.com/vintagehairstyles/category/40s-hairstyles/page/2

"Where a terrible evil is defeated and a Jewish state….."
WC: http://www.internationalwallofprayer.org/A-295-In-Defense-of-Zionist-Movement.html

ADDITIONAL SOURCES

Friedman, Carl. *Nightfather*. New York: Persea Books, 1995.

Hass, Aaron. *In The Shadow of the Holocaust: The Second Generation*. Cambridge: University Press, 2001.

"of delicate hands and bodies burning"

"And as the painted fiend drew the flaming torch….."
Simmons, Gene. *KISS And Make-Up* p. 88. New York: Three Rivers Press, 2002.

"An SS officer cooked a potato over….."
Hass, Aaron. *In The Shadow of the Holocaust: The Second Generation* p. 78. Cambridge: University Press, 2001.

"She remembered, as if it were yesterday, being 14 years old….."
Simmons, Gene. *Sex, Money, KISS* p.21. Beverly Hills: Simmons Books, 2003.

"Chaim Klein was acutely aware that the most….."
Bukiet, Melvin Jules. *Nothing Makes You Free: Writings By Descendants of Jewish Holocaust Sur-*

vivors p. 16. New York: W.W. Norton & Company, Inc., 2002.

"The Mantra 'Never Forget' had been....."
Hass, Aaron. *In The Shadow of the Holocaust: The Second Generation* p. 85. Cambridge: University Press, 2001.

"He only knew that the other children's parents....."
Bukiet, Melvin Jules. *Nothing Makes You Free: Writings By Descendants of Jewish Holocaust Survivors* p. 14. New York: W.W. Norton & Company, Inc., 2002.

"My Mother Is The Most Beautiful Woman In The World....."
Gill, Julian. *The KISS & Related Recordings Focus* p. 21. Sna Francisco: KISSFAQ.com, 2004.

"Flora lived to create a cild called 'Life'....."
Hass, Aaron. *In The Shadow of the Holocaust: The Second Generation* p. 65. Cambridge: University Press, 2001.

"Hitler lost."
Hass, Aaron. *In The Shadow of the Holocaust: The Second Generation* p. 43. Cambridge: University Press, 2001.

"full"

"One day, and I assure you….."
Simmons, Gene. *KISS And Make-Up* p. 120. New York: Three Rivers Press, 2002.

"After a terrifying experience of finding….."
Simmons, Gene. *KISS And Make-Up* p. 20. New York: Three Rivers Press, 2002.

"Chaim! My darling son!"
Goldberg, Danny. *Bumping Into Geniuses* pp.108-109. New York: Penguin Books, 2008.

"dust and clay"

"The slave can become the master. This is….."
Sherwin, Byron L. *Golems Among Us* p.17. Chicago: Ivan R. Dee, 2004

"This was certainly true for the 16th century Rabbi Judah….."
Sherwin, Byron L. *Golems Among Us* p.31. Chicago: Ivan R. Dee, 2004

"At Yeshiva, young Chaim studied….."
Simmons, Gene. *KISS And Make-Up* p. 29. New York: Three Rivers Press, 2002.

"To have somehow created a Golem
that would have protected….."
Beeber, Steven Lee. *The Heebie-Jeebies At CBGB's: A Secret History of Jewish Punk* p. 130. Illinois: Chicago Press Review, Inc., 2006.

"The Golem would have to revert back to….."
Sherwin, Byron L. *Golems Among Us* p.13. Chicago: Ivan R. Dee, 2004.

"As childhood gave way to adolescence, Chaim….."
"Famous Monsters of Filmland" #226, p.21, 1999

"Preparing the 4 inch die cut textured….."
WC: http://www.threatricalmakeupsupplies.com/spongestools.php

"Kaolinite clay and dipped his latex….."
WC: http://www.blushweb.com/mineral-make-up/ingredients.htm

"A life-form created from dust and clay….."
Sherwin, Byron L. *Golems Among Us* p.8. Chicago: Ivan R. Dee, 2004.

"On the occasions it would terrorize and drench it's underlings….."
Konow, David. *Bang Your Head: The Rise And Fall of Heavy Metal* p. 63. New York: Three Rivers Press, 2002.

"To the blackened finger-smeared jars of clay and chipped….."
WC: http://calstaging.bemidjistate.edu/studnets/kkritzeck/howto.html

ADDITIONAL SOURCES
Chabon, Michael. *The Amazing Adventures of Kavalier & Clay*. New York: Picador, 2000.

Zusak, Markus. *The Book Thief*. New York: Borzoi Books, 2005.

"flashpots and talcum powder"

"By 1974, the members of KISS had been….." Gooch, Curt and Jeff Suhs. *KISS Alive Forever: The Complete Touring History* p.32. New York: Billboard Books, 2002.

"Gene put his arm around Flora and gently….." Bernstein, Fred A. *The Jewish Mother's Hall of Fame* p. 140. New York: Doubleday & Company, Inc., 1986.

ADDITIONAL SOURCES

Epstein, Helen. *Children of the Holocaust: Conversations with Sons and Daughters of Survivors*. New

York: Penguin Books, 1988.

Spiegelman, Art. *Maus*. New York: Pantheon Books, 1986.

"a twinship"

"Many years before circumstances in Terre Haute….."
WC: http://web.indstate.edu/vchs/thisisit.htm

"You see, no is only no….."
WC: http://www.genesimmons.com

"As a boy, Chaim Witz doggedly….…"
Simmons, Gene. *Sex, Money, KISS* p.23. Beverly Hills: Simmons Books, 2003.

"He wrote songs and consigned them to….."
Stanley, Paul and Gene Simmons. *KISSTORY* p. 11. Los Angeles: KISSTORY Ltd., 1994

"As a young adult, Gene Simmons harvested….."
Stanley, Paul and Gene Simmons. *KISSTORY* p. 3. Los Angeles: KISSTORY Ltd., 1994

"Lifeguard….."
Simmons, Gene. *KISS And Make-Up* p. 52. New York: Three Rivers Press, 2002.

"Paper Boy….."
Gene Simmons on <u>Shrink Rap with Pamela Stephenson</u>',UK: Channel Four. Episode Eight; 28 April 2008.

"Publisher's Assistant….."
Duncan, Robert. *KISS* p. 34. New York: Popular Library, 1978.

"Grade School Teacher….."
Lendt, C.K. *KISS And Sell: The Making of a Supergroup* p.41. New York: Billboard Books, 1997.

"He purchased equipment then rented it out….."
Simmons, Gene. *Sex, Money, KISS* p.44. Beverly Hills: Simmons Books, 2003.

"His discipline and savings allowed for a pivotal….."
Duncan, Robert. *KISS* p. 34. New York: Popular Library, 1978.

"Transportation to and from….."
Simmons, Gene. *KISS And Make-Up* p. 73. New York: Three Rivers Press, 2002.

"You guys better start playing some KISS records….."
WC: <u>http://www.indstate.edu/iq/Geek_Issue/Kiss_Army.htm</u>

"Like the one that allowed mild-mannered reporter….."
Weinstein, Rabbi Simcha. *Up, Up, And Oy Vey: How Jewish History, Culture, and Values Shaped the Comic Book Superhero* p.21. Maryland: Leviathon Press, 2006.

"Like the one that allowed a laid back, humble high…..
WC: http://www.indstate.edu/iq/Geek_Issue/Kiss_Army.htm

"Another Jew – courtesy of his mother's genealogical….."
Nash, Alanna and Billy Smith and Marty Lacker and Lamar Fike. *Elvis Aaron Presley: Revelations From The Memphis Mafia* p. 3. New York: Harper Collins, 1995.
WC: http://www.elvisinfonet.com/schmelvis.html

"A fascination to humankind since the first set….."
WC: http://www.aboutbibleprophecy.com/p98.htm

"The CANDLES Museum. Short for….."
WC: http://www.candlesholocaustmuseum.org/index.php?sid=3

"For his pioneering spirit, Bill Starkey was presented a plaque….."
WC: http://www.indstate.edu/iq/Geek_Issue/Kiss_

Army.htm

"The stench of Mengele's deeds; so deeply foul….."
Posner, Gerald L. and John Ware. *Mengele: The Complete Story* p.34. New York: McGraw-Hill Book Company, 1986.

"Amputating their limbs and stuffing wood shavings….."
Posner, Gerald L. and John Ware. *Mengele: The Complete Story* p.79. New York: McGraw-Hill Book Company, 1986.

"Sewing separate bodies together….."
Posner, Gerald L. and John Ware. *Mengele: The Complete Story* p.37. New York: McGraw-Hill Book Company, 1986.

"Live autopsies. Shock….."
Posner, Gerald L. and John Ware. *Mengele: The Complete Story* p.324. New York: McGraw-Hill Book Company, 1986.

"He burned children alive in giant….."
Posner, Gerald L. and John Ware. *Mengele: The Complete Story* p.45. New York: McGraw-Hill Book Company, 1986.

"When the war ended, the once omnipotent….."

WC: http://www.ushmm.org/wlc/en/article.php?ModuleId=10007060

"if i look lost"

"I've got a new rock group for you, Totie", talk show….."
Kissology. Perf: Peter Criss, Ace Frehley, Gene Simmons, and Paul Stanley. DVD, 2006.

"They bullied and they laughed….."
Gene Simmons on Shrink Rap with Pamela Stephenson',UK: Channel Four. Episode Eight; 28 April 2008.

"If I look lost, point me….."
Leaf, David and Ken Sharp. *KISS – Behind The Mask: The Official Authorized Biography* p. 316. New York: Warner Books, 2003.

"He excelled at the non-verbal game of….."
Simmons, Gene. *KISS And Make-Up* p. 23. New York: Three Rivers Press, 2002.

"So, what are you supposed to be?" asked a perplexed….."
Kissology. Perf: Peter Criss, Ace Frehley, Gene Simmons, and Paul Stanley. DVD, 2006.

"He would amount to being the biggest….."

Swenson, John. *Headliners: KISS* p. 100. New York: Grosset & Dunlap, Inc., 1978.

"tuesdays with stan lee"

"There is a point of discussion I would like….."
Leaf, David and Ken Sharp. *KISS – Behind The Mask: The Official Authorized Biography* p. 160. New York: Warner Books, 2003.

"What was the creative spark behind the double-page….."
Benton, Mike. *The Illustrated History: Superhero Comics of the Golden Age* p. 85. Texas: Taylor Publishing Company, 1992.

"The decade that introduced Batman, Robin….."
Benton, Mike. *The Illustrated History: Superhero Comics of the Golden Age* pp. 13-27. Texas: Taylor Publishing Company, 1992.

"Three decades. The forties. The fifties….."
Kaplan, Arie. *From Krakow To Krypton* p. 63. Philadelphia: The Jewish Publication Society, 2008.

"Okay, Stan…..Superman 12. Page….." Leaf, David and Ken Sharp. *KISS – Behind The Mask: The Official Authorized Biography* p. 60. New York: Warner Books, 2003.

"Created by two Jews in the 1930's, the Man of….."
Weinstein, Rabbi Simcha. *Up, Up, And Oy Vey: How Jewish History, Culture, and Values Shaped the Comic Book Superhero* p.21. Maryland: Leviathon Press, 2006.

"He was the quintessential American….."
Kaplan, Arie. *From Krakow To Krypton* p. 24. Philadelphia: The Jewish Publication Society, 2008.

"His real name was Kal-El, meaning….."
Kaplan, Arie. *From Krakow To Krypton* p. 14. Philadelphia: The Jewish Publication Society, 2008.

"Kal-El's parents placed him in a vessel….."
Weinstein, Rabbi Simcha. *Up, Up, And Oy Vey: How Jewish History, Culture, and Values Shaped the Comic Book Superhero* p.24. Maryland: Leviathon Press, 2006.

"Both Kal-El and Moses were discovered by….."
Weinstein, Rabbi Simcha. *Up, Up, And Oy Vey: How Jewish History, Culture, and Values Shaped the Comic Book Superhero* p.27. Maryland: Leviathon Press, 2006.

"Just as the Golem was created to defend….."
Kaplan, Arie. *From Krakow To Krypton* p. 15. Philadelphia: The Jewish Publication Society, 2008.

"Before becoming Batman, Bruce Wayne….."
Weinstein, Rabbi Simcha. *Up, Up, And Oy Vey: How Jewish History, Culture, and Values Shaped the Comic Book Superhero* p.37. Maryland: Leviathon Press, 2006.

"Batman went on to battle….."
Weinstein, Rabbi Simcha. *Up, Up, And Oy Vey: How Jewish History, Culture, and Values Shaped the Comic Book Superhero* p.38. Maryland: Leviathon Press, 2006.

"Captain Marvel Jr. took on Captain Nazi….."
Nash, Alanna and Billy Smith and Marty Lacker and Lamar Fike. *Elvis Aaron Presley: Revelations From The Memphis Mafia* p. 506. New York: Harper Collins, 1995.

"And the Nazi poundings continued….."
Weinstein, Rabbi Simcha. *Up, Up, And Oy Vey: How Jewish History, Culture, and Values Shaped the Comic Book Superhero* pp. 64-66. Maryland: Leviathon Press, 2006.

"The Hulk and The Thing were….."
Kaplan, Arie. *From Krakow To Krypton* p. 109. Philadelphia: The Jewish Publication Society, 2008.

"Spiderman and Peter Parker suffered guilt….."
Weinstein, Rabbi Simcha. *Up, Up, And Oy Vey: How Jewish History, Culture, and Values Shaped*

the Comic Book Superhero p 99. Maryland: Leviathon Press, 2006.

"In 1939, Superman fought to keep….."
Weinstein, Rabbi Simcha. *Up, Up, And Oy Vey: How Jewish History, Culture, and Values Shaped the Comic Book Superhero* pp. 25-28. Maryland: Leviathon Press, 2006.

"Gene Simmons. Comic Book Superhero. This was….."
Leaf, David and Ken Sharp. *KISS – Behind The Mask: The Official Authorized Biography* p. 161. New York: Warner Books, 2003.

"Thrilled by the spectacle he….."
Simmons, Gene. *KISS And Make-Up* p. 40. New York: Three Rivers Press, 2002.

"In Junior High School, another glow….."
Simmons, Gene. *KISS And Make-Up* p. 38. New York: Three Rivers Press, 2002.

"Stan, when I was a kid I wrote you….."
Simmons, Gene. *KISS And Make-Up* p. 136. New York: Three Rivers Press, 2002.

"mazel tov"
"We played four nights at Budokan and broke attendance….."

Simmons, Gene. *KISS And Make-Up* p. 133. New York: Three Rivers Press, 2002.

"T-shirts. Necklaces. Posters. Tour Books. Belt….."
Swenson, John. *Headliners: KISS* p. 173. New York: Grosset & Dunlap, Inc., 1978.

"We'll be adapting the KISS comic book storyline for our first….."
Swenson, John. *Headliners: KISS* p. 169. New York: Grosset & Dunlap, Inc., 1978.

"Four solo albums released at the same….."
Swenson, John. *Headliners: KISS* p. 172. New York: Grosset & Dunlap, Inc., 1978.

"And we were just voted the top rock band in….."
Swenson, John. *Headliners: KISS* p. 165. New York: Grosset & Dunlap, Inc., 1978.

"Last night on the plane I was talking to management about something….."
Kissology. Perf: Peter Criss, Ace Frehley, Gene Simmons, and Paul Stanley. DVD, 2006.

"I am so proud. So what else are you….."
Simmons, Gene. *Sex, Money, KISS* p. 22. Beverly Hills: Simmons Books, 2003.

"never forget to remember"

"Zeig Heil!", the man yelled, dressed in Nazi….."
Gebert, Gordon G.G. and Bob McAdams. *KISS & Tell* p. 39. New York: Pitbull Publishing, 1997.

"And walking up Madison Avenue to
60th, Flora arrived every week….."
Lendt, C.K. *KISS And Sell: The Making of a Supergroup* p.42. New York: Billboard Books, 1997.

"Did they realize that long ago the Jews were forced….."
Altman, Linda Jacobs. *The Importance of Simon Wiesenthal* p. 21. New York: Lucent Books, 2000.

"In the camps, she had spent her days fishing lunch….."
WC: http://www.genesimmons.com

"When his black and white world….."
Swenson, John. *Headliners: KISS* p. 39. New York: Grosset & Dunlap, Inc., 1978.

"There could be more but only if he….."
Simmons, Gene. *Sex, Money, KISS* p. 212. Beverly Hills: Simmons Books, 2003.

"And most of them realized it. Most of them recognized that the sturdy SS Man's….." Spiegelman,

Art. *Maus* p. 71. New York: Pantheon Books, 1986.

Power. Money. Influence. Control….."
Hass, Aaron. *In The Shadow of the Holocaust: The Second Generation* p. 61. Cambridge: University Press, 2001.

"How to live inside an armor shell….."
WC: http://www.genesimmons.com

ADDITIONAL SOURCES
Criss, Lydia. *Sealed With A Kiss*. New York: Buccaneer Books, 2006.

"like the blur of a skater goes round and round"

"At the Glickman/Marks Management office….."
Lendt, C.K. *KISS And Sell: The Making of a Supergroup* p.41. New York: Billboard Books, 1997.

"In 2011, Gene visited his father's gravesite in Israel……"
"Blood Is Thicker Than Hummus": Gene Simmons Family Jewels', Arts & Entertainment Network. Season Six, Episode Fifteen; 28 June 2011.

"I KNOW GENE SIMMONS PERSONALLY"
People Magazine, 4/10/78, Volume 9; Number 14

"Attending one of Cher's annual skating parties….."
Goldmine Magazine, 1996; Number 6

"At age 27, he was in love for the first….."
People Magazine, 10/22/79, Volume 12; Number 17

"Gene, along with 74 million other people, had watched….."
Lennon, Cynthia. *John* p. 134. New York: Crown Publishers, 2005.

"Heck, the members of KISS had their faces patented….."
Stanley, Paul and Gene Simmons. *KISSTORY* p. 3. Los Angeles: KISSTORY Ltd., 1994.

"Does KISS really stand for Knights in Satan's….."
Simmons, Gene. *KISS And Make-Up* p. 119. New York: Three Rivers Press, 2002.

"Uh, excuse me guys – I've enjoyed….."
Goldmine Magazine, 1996; Number 6

"Cher was replaced by a lovely Supreme….."
Lendt, C.K. *KISS And Sell: The Making of a Supergroup* p.186. New York: Billboard Books, 1997.

"Shining brightest on three brothers called Gibb. Seven….."
Cook, Hector and Andrew Mon Hughes and Me-

linda Bilyeu. *The Ultimate Biography of the Bee Gees: Tales of the Brothers Gibb* p. 420. London: Omnibus Press, 2003.

"And in the darkness of the movie theatre, Gene watched....."
WC: Mirror.co.uk 3/5/10

"To the rest of the world he was the God....."
Simmons, Gene. *KISS And Make-Up* p. 221. New York: Three Rivers Press, 2002.

"passover"

"A roasted egg hardened under....."
Schweitzer, Rabbi Peter H. *The Liberated Haggadah* p. 24-27. New York: The Center For Cultural Judasim, 2003.

"Gene – as the man of the house – sat at....."
Simmons, Gene. *Sex, Money, KISS* p. 81. Beverly Hills: Simmons Books, 2003.

"It was the story that Jesus told....."
WC: http://www.herealittletherealittle.net

"The Book of Exodus commands it. It commands....."
Gubkin, Liora. *You Shall Tell Your Children* p. 21. New Brunswick: Rutgers University Press, 2007.

"But even in the death camps, prisoners found….."
Ganor, Solly. *Passover In Dauchau*
WC: www.chgs.umn/edu/histories/documentary/ganorPassover.pdf, 2007.

"The will to bear witness….."
Gubkin, Liora. *You Shall Tell Your Children* p. 63. New Brunswick: Rutgers University Press, 2007.

"Flora returned to her childhood home….."
Spiegelman, Art. *Maus II: A Survivor's Tale* p. 50. New York: Pantheon Books, 1991.

"Flora found a new home….."
KISS Crazy #4, UK Fanzine

"passover"

"Television host Tom Snyder was a strange cross….."
WC: http://www.BestWeekEver.TV/2007-07-30/tom-snyders-greatest-rockmoments/

"Gene sat through the whole of the interview brooding….."
Kissology. Perf: Peter Criss, Ace Frehley, Gene Simmons, and Paul Stanley. DVD, 2006.

"Symphonies. Time pieces. Architecture….."

WC: http://www.germanculture.com.ua/

"Pillows and mattresses were stuffed….."
WC: http://answers.yahoo.com/questions/
index?qid=80516163709AAjiTT2

"Lampshades were made from human….."
WC: http://www.scrapbookpages.com/Dachau/
scrapbook/DachauTrials/llseKoch.html

"Human fat was rendered into bars of….."
WC: http://www.straightdope.com

"The soldiers photographed it all….."
Klee, Ernst and Willi Dressen and Volker Reiss
The Good Old Days: The Holocaust As Seen By Its Perpetrators And Bystanders p. xx. New York: Konecky and Konecky, 1991.

"The men and women. Naked. Humiliated….."
Night And Fog. Dir. Alain Resnais. Film. Janus, 1955.

"And yet - let us not overlook the advantages of….."
WC: http://wiki.answers.com/Q/What_were_the_Nazi_countries

"We were just following orders….."
Klee, Ernst and Willi Dressen and Volker Reiss

The Good Old Days: The Holocaust As Seen By Its Perpetrators And Bystanders p. 73. New York: Konecky and Konecky, 1991.

"We were just regular townsfolk. We didn't….."
Klee, Ernst and Willi Dressen and Volker Reiss *The Good Old Days: The Holocaust As Seen By Its Perpetrators And Bystanders* p. xx. New York: Konecky and Konecky, 1991.

"As soldiers, we had no choice. They would have killed….."
Klee, Ernst and Willi Dressen and Volker Reiss *The Good Old Days: The Holocaust As Seen By Its Perpetrators And Bystanders* p. xiii. New York: Konecky and Konecky, 1991.

"We know that the townsfolk reduced the Jews to pulp….."
Klee, Ernst and Willi Dressen and Volker Reiss *The Good Old Days: The Holocaust As Seen By Its Perpetrators And Bystanders* p. 31. New York: Konecky and Konecky, 1991.

"The murder of Jews in the city streets increasingly….."
Klee, Ernst and Willi Dressen and Volker Reiss *The Good Old Days: The Holocaust As Seen By Its Perpetrators And Bystanders* p. xx. New York: Konecky and Konecky, 1991.

"We know from official written orders, countless….."
Klee, Ernst and Willi Dressen and Volker Reiss
The Good Old Days: The Holocaust As Seen By Its Perpetrators And Bystanders pp. 76-77. New York: Konecky and Konecky, 1991.

"In fact, as ruthless as the Nazis were to their….."
Klee, Ernst and Willi Dressen and Volker Reiss
The Good Old Days: The Holocaust As Seen By Its Perpetrators And Bystanders p. 82. New York: Konecky and Konecky, 1991.

"Nazi officers were endlessly refining the killing process….."
Klee, Ernst and Willi Dressen and Volker Reiss
The Good Old Days: The Holocaust As Seen By Its Perpetrators And Bystanders p. 114. New York: Konecky and Konecky, 1991.

"It was decided that Gas-Vans would be used to….."
Klee, Ernst and Willi Dressen and Volker Reiss
The Good Old Days: The Holocaust As Seen By Its Perpetrators And Bystanders p. 73. New York: Konecky and Konecky, 1991.

"Perhaps large 'shower facilities' filled with….."
Klee, Ernst and Willi Dressen and Volker Reiss
The Good Old Days: The Holocaust As Seen By Its Perpetrators And Bystanders p. 74. New York: Konecky and Konecky, 1991.

"the writhing surface of the ocean's skin"

"The painted warrior shot flames into the air….."
Duncan, Robert. *KISS* pp. 24-25. New York: Popular Library, 1978.

"His new bride - - a jubilant middle-aged woman with heavy Hungarian….."
Simmons, Gene. *KISS And Make-Up* INSERT 1. New York: Three Rivers Press, 2002.

"the elder"

"The final waft of cancerous vapor….."
WC: http://www.healthliteracy.worlded.org/docs/tobacco/Unit4/3other_health.html

"Tweed jacket; nestling deep within….."
WC: http://www.britannica.com/facts/5/359389/polyester-as-discussed-in-textile

"A female associate in purple polyester….."
WC: http://www.whatispolyester.com/

"It had been a mere three years….."
Lendt, C.K. *KISS And Sell: The Making of a Supergroup* p.233. New York: Billboard Books, 1997.

"Bouncing off his synapse tubes….."

WC: http://en.wikipedia.org/wiki/Cerebellum

"Setting: a post-apocalyptic world nearly….."
Stanley, Paul and Gene Simmons. *KISSTORY* p. 313. Los Angeles: KISSTORY Ltd., 1994

"He began to ebb and flow upon a sea….."
WC: http://www.formulaformiracles.net/brain-waves.html

"Renowned rock producer Bob Ezrin….."
Lendt, C.K. *KISS And Sell: The Making of a Supergroup* p.234. New York: Billboard Books, 1997.

"The American Symphony Orchestra and St. Robert's Choir….."
Lendt, C.K. *KISS And Sell: The Making of a Supergroup* p.239. New York: Billboard Books, 1997.

"Aucoin explained to the group that….."
Lendt, C.K. *KISS And Sell: The Making of a Supergroup* p.237. New York: Billboard Books, 1997.

"From the initial strains….."
Lendt, C.K. *KISS And Sell: The Making of a Supergroup* p.239. New York: Billboard Books, 1997.

"They re-sequenced the songs….."
Lendt, C.K. *KISS And Sell: The Making of a Supergroup* p.240. New York: Billboard Books, 1997.

"In the end – KISS lost fans, Polygram….."
Lendt, C.K. *KISS And Sell: The Making of a Supergroup* p.241. New York: Billboard Books, 1997.

ADDITIONAL SOURCES
Sherman, Dale. *Black Diamond: The Unauthorized Biography of KISS*. London: CG Publishing Ltd., 1997.

"in flight"

"Her decision to conclude….."
WC:http://www.chron.com/channel/momhouston/commons/hotflashes.html?plckController=Blog&plckScript=blogScript&plckElementId=blogDest&plckBlogPage=BlogViewPost&plckPostId=Blog%3aeb23504d-4773-45d6-a28c-8c54c8b-b0bbaPost%3a91dc5d93-a104-4fa3-a518-ba0d-09b33a32

"Flora turned toward the window. She began….."
Gill, Julian. *The KISS Album Focus* p. 19. San Francisco: KISSFAQ.COM, 2002.

"The elaborate complex of Registry….."
WC: http://www.yale.edu/ynhti/curriculum/units/1999/3/99.03.01.x.html

"Eyelids were everted and checked for….."

WC: http://www.ellisisland.org/genealogy/ellis_island_history.asp

"For a moment she trembled as she….."
WC: http://www.jewishvirtuallibrary.org/jsource/Politics/embassy.html

"Flora closed her eyes, felt the rumblings….."
'Face Your Demons: <u>Gene Simmons Family Jewels</u>', Arts & Entertainment Network. Season Six, Episode One; 5 December 2010.

"Here is my business card….."   WC:http://www.chron.com/channel/momhouston/commons/hotflashes.html?plckController=Blog&plckScript=blogScript&plckElementId=blogDest&plckBlogPage=BlogViewPost&plckPostId=Blog%3aeb23504d-4773-45d6-a28c-8c54c8bb0bbaPost%3a91dc5d93-a104-4fa3-a518-ba0d09b33a32

<u>ADDITIONAL SOURCES</u>
Frankl, Viktor E. *Man's Search For Meaning*. Boston: Beacon Press, 1992.

"zimmerman & klein"

"Folk singer Robert Zimmerman….."
Heylin, Clinton. *Bob Dylan: Behind The Shades Revisited* p. 47. New York: Harper Collins, Inc., 2001

"A decade later he began to….."
Heylin, Clinton. *Bob Dylan: Behind The Shades Revisited* p. 517. New York: Harper Collins, Inc., 2001

"Interestingly, not only would Dylan….."
Heylin, Clinton. *Bob Dylan: Behind The Shades Revisited* p. 590. New York: Harper Collins, Inc., 2001

"He also went on to adopt Gene's….."
WC: http://www.genesimmons.com

"One afternoon, Gene called Bob….."
WC: http://www.genesimmons.com

ADDITIONAL SOURCES
Harris, Larry and Curt Gooch and Jeff Suhs. *And Party Every Day: The Inside Story of Casablanca Records*. New York: Backbeat Books, 2009.

Tweed, Shannon and Julie McCarron. *KISS And Tell*. Beverly Hills: Simmons Books, 2006.

"smothered and abandoned"

"At Elmhurst Newtown High School, the 33rd….."
WC: http://www.kissasylum.com, 2006.

"The old gymnasium had been spruced up with balloons….."

WC: http://www.ehow.com/way_5370779_tips-planning-high-school-reunion

"Tunes like 'Kind of a Drag' and….."
WC: http://www.musicoutfitters.com/topsongs/1967/htm

"Sena Rosenberg and Phyllis….."
WC: http://www.kissasylum.com, 2006.

"Fame and its magical powers….."
Redmond, Sean and Su Holmes. *Stardom And Celebrity* p. 81. Los Angeles: Sage Publications, 2007.

"That the famous individual is legitimate. He must….."
Redmond, Sean and Su Holmes. *Stardom And Celebrity* p. 82. Los Angeles: Sage Publications, 2007.

"Fame proves to the world….."
Schickel, Richard. *Intimate Strangers: The Culture of Celebrity* p. 130. New York: Doubleday & Company, Inc., 1985.

"Gene's early years in America were marked by being bullied….."
'Gene Simmons on Shrink Rap with Pamela Stephenson',UK: Channel Four. Episode Eight; 28 April 2008.

"Winning a dance contest in school, but….."
Swenson, John. *Headliners: KISS* p. 40. New York: Grosset & Dunlap, Inc., 1978.

"At camp, Gene's first foray into singing was….."
Simmons, Gene. *KISS And Make-Up* p. 48. New York: Three Rivers Press, 2002.

"At Roosevelt Jr. High School, Gene was set to….."
'KISStastrophe: <u>Gene Simmons Family Jewels</u>', Arts & Entertainment Network. Season Five, Episode Four; 4 April 2010.

"After graduating from Richmond College, Gene set out to find….." Swenson, John. *Headliners: KISS* p. 19. New York: Grosset & Dunlap, Inc., 1978.

"And like so many other individuals who later succeed in….."
Giles, David. *Illusions of Immortality: A Psychology of Fame and Celebrity* p. 14. New York: MacMillan Press Ltd., 2000.

"Fame was the goal; the vehicle….."
Giles, David. *Illusions of Immortality: A Psychology of Fame and Celebrity* p. 35. New York: MacMillan Press Ltd., 2000.

"On reflection, Gene Simmons was both abandoned and….."

Giles, David. *Illusions of Immortality: A Psychology of Fame and Celebrity* p. 40. New York: MacMillan Press Ltd., 2000.

"'I'll show them'. The mantra….."
WC: http://www.theocentric.com/culture/issues/fame_junkies.html, 2008.

"He needed to transform the world into the role of….."
WC: http://www.wehaitians.com/thefamemotive.html, 2006.

"The risk of public humiliation in the spotlight….."
Simmons, Gene. *KISS And Make-Up* p. 58. New York: Three Rivers Press, 2002.

"For the chance to discard the past….."
Redmond, Sean and Su Holmes. *Stardom And Celebrity* p. 183. Los Angeles: Sage Publications, 2007.

"For the chance to soothe the wounds of….."
Schickel, Richard. *Intimate Strangers: The Culture of Celebrity* p. 18. New York: Doubleday & Company, Inc., 1985.

ADDITIONAL SOURCES
Caplan, Lincoln. *The Insanity Defense and The Trial of John W. Hinckley, Jr.* Boston: Godine Publisher, Inc., 1984.

Low, Peter W. and John Calvin Jeffires, Jr. and Richard J. Bonnie. *The Trial of John W. Hinckley, Jr.: A Case Study in the Insanity Defense*. New York: The Foundation Press, Inc., 1986.

"a return to israel"
"53 years since he had last….."
WC: http://www.genesimmons.com

"Yad Vashem Holocaust Museum, located….."
WC: http://www.yadvashem.org/

"A bus exploded. Off in the….."
WC: http://www.genesimmons.com

ADDITIONAL SOURCES

Friedman, Carl. *Nightfather*. New York: Persea Books, 1995.

Hass, Aaron. *In The Shadow of the Holocaust: The Second Generation*. Cambridge: University Press, 2001.

"childhood's end"
"His trip to New York had been anything….."
WC: http://www.genesimmons.com

"Hi, my name is Gene. I used to….."
'Kisstastrophe: <u>Gene Simmons Family Jewels</u>', Arts & Entertainment Network. Season 5, Episode 6; 18 April 2010.

"To the home where he had kept a diary….."
Simmons, Gene. *KISS And Make-Up* p. 51. New York: Three Rivers Press, 2002.

"Channel 9's 'Million Dollar Movie' showcasing….."
Swenson, John. *Headliners: KISS* p. 38. New York: Grosset & Dunlap, Inc., 1978.

"Had first seen The Beatles perform on….."
Simmons, Gene. *KISS And Make-Up* p. 38. New York: Three Rivers Press, 2002.

"The tour ended with….."
'Kisstastrophe: <u>Gene Simmons Family Jewels</u>', Arts & Entertainment Network. Season 5, Episode 6; 18 April 2010.

"plenty of time to rest"
"A lilting drone to take the place of….."
Leaf, David and Ken Sharp. *KISS – Behind The Mask: The Official Authorized Biography* p. 408. New York: Warner Books, 2003.

"It was so like America. The whirling….."
'Gene Simmons on <u>Shrink Rap with Pamela</u>

Stephenson',UK: Channel Four. Episode Eight; 28 April 2008.

"The leather clad beast in warpaint and….." Duncan, Robert. KISS p. 24. New York: Popular Library, 1978.

ADDITIONAL SOURCES
Epstein, Helen. *Children of the Holocaust: Conversations with Sons and Daughters of Survivors.* New York: Penguin Books, 1988.

Hass, Aaron. *In The Shadow of the Holocaust: The Second Generation.* Cambridge: University Press, 2001.

Spiegelman, Art. Maus. New York: Pantheon Books, 1986.

about the author

Ross Berg has been a Gene Simmons/KISS fanatic for 35 years. He worked for many years as a Moderator for KISSonline – the band's official website – prior to creating 'The Flora Army', which was featured on the A&E Television Series "Gene Simmons Family Jewels". He has had the pleasure of meeting Gene Simmons three times, Nick Tweed-Simmons during a special unveiling of his debut comic book, and is followed by Miss Shannon Tweed on his 'Flora Army' Twitter site. A large collection of rare Fanzines created by Gene Klein from the 1960's serve as the crown jewel in the extensive museum of KISS merchandise Ross has collected since the age of seven. Ross Berg holds a Master's Degree and lives in California with his beautiful wife and two loving children.

CPSIA information can be obtained at www.ICGtesting.com
Printed in the USA
BVOW032353161012

303202BV00001B/7/P